This book is for you if...

- you believe you've got what it takes to succeed – but need someone to open the door;

- you are ready to make a positive change in your life;

- you are not satisfied with the 'status quo' and want more from life;

- you have seen others succeed in property and want to know how to do the same;

- you have a big vision for the future and need a mentor to get you there;

- you want to know the <u>one</u> question that made me a millionaire; and,

- you know you don't know what you don't know.

"However difficult life may seem, there is always something you can do and succeed at."

Stephen Hawking

What people are saying about Glenn

"Four incredible days spent with the 'negotiating ninja', Glenn has an ability to make something seem so left field. Such a light-bulb moment. My head is scrambled with knowledge that I must put in place to reach my financial goal. My background is managing a photography studio; I am an amateur investor who has been taught to follow the conventional method. This would never get me to where I want to get to within the time constraints. Thank you to Glenn, Tony, Steve and Mel. Here's to a great working future."

Grant

"I am an ex-builder/property maintenance, but not working for customers anymore. I'm concentrating on managing and expanding my portfolio, and will be systemising everything. I loved the course as it was more personal than all the other courses I have been on."

Philip Lacey

"I am a relatively new investor and found the days very interesting. It gave me the feedback of new ideas."

Oliver Musgrave

"I am an amateur property professional. I have known for over 12 months that I will make property/developments and investments my career, hobby and passion for life. I am employed full-time as a designer and have now started a small architectural business. I will leave my job in January 2016 and start my mentorship then, if not sooner, dependent on my time between now and then."

Stefan Gavin

"I am a property investor of eight to nine years, currently running and working within three businesses and running my own property portfolio. I was sceptical about coming on this course but my view has changed and I really enjoyed the education Glenn and his staff have provided. It has given me a royal kick up the backside as I believe we are sitting on some extremely interesting and potential deals. I would strongly recommend Glenn's courses, and wish to thank you all for the experience."

Nathan McAlindon

"I'm an ex-location/production manager, and now full-time property investor in London and Birmingham.

"The phrase 'you don't know what you don't know' has never been truer than this weekend. I've been gobsmacked by the volume, relevance and practicality of the strategies on offer this weekend. I have built up a good store of knowledge and strategies over the last three years, but this four-day course has opened my eyes to a whole new realm of possibility within my grasps.

"I cannot recommend this course highly enough; full of intelligent, practical, real-world information. A whole new buffet of strategies to pick from. Thank you, Glenn and the team."

"I wish I had attended this course 10 years ago. Mind-blowing."

Christina Brown

What Glenn's mentees are saying

Juswant and Sylvia Rai

We met Glenn in 2005 and became aware that he's a very active property investor. Since then, he's gone on to be a prolific investor on an even larger scale! Glenn enjoys working with people who can make things happen and have the drive to succeed. If you're one of those people, Glenn is the guy to go to! There's very little he doesn't know about investing in property in the UK, and he loves helping people move forward and achieve their goals.

When I first went to one of his events, I remember him saying, "I fully expect most of you not to do anything as a result of this event, because that's human nature. You'll come here, you'll have a great day, and you'll learn loads. The question is, are you one of those people who is willing to take action? At the end of the day, it doesn't really matter what you learn if you don't apply it."

He challenged people to put an advert in their local paper looking for properties for sale and to send him a copy of it to show that they were committed. So we did just that and showed him we were serious. We have never looked back.

There are so many different ways to make money in property – it's like being a kid in a candy store! However, if you don't know where to focus your efforts, you can waste a lot of time and money. Glenn helps us to refine our goals and select the right strategies for us.

I find it fascinating how people find it easy to spend a thousand pounds on a TV that's going to sit in a corner sending them into a coma, rather than spending a thousand pounds investing in their education to find out how to create a sustainable business and to generate wealth.

Over the last decade, we have attended several of Glenn's courses, and he has helped us with BMV sourcing and negotiation with estate agents. In addition to this, we have managed to build up a HMO portfolio and R2R income by ourselves, which means we bring in income from properties and assets that we do not own but that we control.

We have a property business now and neither of us work full-time for anybody else.

Glenn has been a supportive friend and has been kind enough to take time out to help and guide us whenever we've needed it.

Des Taylor

My background is in recruitment and IT, and I have grown a big network of contacts over the years. When I ran a business travel company in the past, I came across Glenn as one of my clients. A few years later, I came across him again when he was running a one-day course on property close to where I lived, so I registered to find out more.

I had previously attended a property seminar in the USA and quickly formed the opinion that the presenters there were great at selling, but no credibility as property investors themselves and no portfolio to prove it. In general, Glenn is very different. Not only had he created a multi-million property empire himself, but he had also helped over 69 people to become equity millionaires in their own right. He both talked the talk and walked the walk. He had achieved a lot and knew what he was talking about.

After the one-day event, I realised that I needed to know more so I enrolled on his four-day course. I was hooked! Glenn looked at my personal qualities and background, and recommended a strategy that was right for me in the rental marketplace for me to achieve the best I can.

I wanted to make a real success of my new property business so I decided to be completely thorough in everything I did. I spent a lot of time doing research, investigating, double-checking, fully understanding licensing, and taxation, We started to look at properties, booking four to five appointments a day. By the time I had viewed a hundred properties in three to four months and still not committed to one of them, I realised I was paralysed by the research. One conversation with Glenn got me back on track and we went back and bought one of the very first properties I had viewed. No matter how much knowledge you have, there is no substitute for working with a mentor who know his stuff.

I think what held me back at the start was a fear of doing the wrong thing and making mistakes, but if you make things happen and take action, results always follow.

However, all my research had given me an insight into a new property trend which presented me with a clear direction for my business. I had noticed that many people were having difficulties getting onto the property ladder, and because of the financial situations that they were in, many found it a real challenge to get their first mortgage.

I could see a need for rented accommodation which had more of an emphasis in living as a small community as well as an emphasis on community spaces in a property to enable people to socialise with their housemates. The way we live is changing.

I believe we're going to see more eating out, more communal eating facilities, something between what we see as food courts and what we see as restaurants, so those groups of people can come together without having to decide on a particular type of food. I think that's coming. I think that will come into the communities as we go forward. I do see this with the tenants in the houses. They do bring their friends together to have dinner, because it's easier than going to a restaurant.

For me, this new style of living has to have a number of factors. One is that they have to be the right configuration. The second thing is that they have to have had an owner or a management company that's happy to do what's necessary to upgrade the properties into what is needed for regulations that exist today, or may exist in the near future.

In today's evolving housing market, there are many opportunities for innovation and in providing accommodation for the way people are now living.

At that time, and to this day, I have a very highly-paid job which means I have to be very efficient with my use of time. But a word of caution – this isn't for you if you don't want to do any work!

However, it is for you if you're tired of going to work nine-to-five and want to grow something amazing and grow a residual income. It is for you if you actually want to realise what it's like to have money coming in that's working for you, rather than you working for the money. I am my money's employer, and I absolutely love that.

My property business allows me to do things I've never been able to do before and gives me access to people, places and things I've never been able to see, but the greatest thing it's given me is time with my family.

For me, it took a little bit longer than it should have done, but I persevered and made it. There is no reason why you cannot do the same – if you take all the advice you are given.

Ian Lawson

As with many of Glenn's private property clients, I was already enjoying a successful career in property before we knew each other. I had built up a substantial portfolio before the market crashed in 2007. I then sold three million of it, leaving me with a portfolio of £5 million and retired to the Caribbean. My partner and I travelled the world for four years, managing the business from our laptops with our local staff managing things on the ground. But you can only travel for so long. I was missing the cut and thrust, and the passion, so in 2011 I decided to get back into the property game.

To get back into the market and to find out where the opportunities were, I looked around for who was at the cutting edge of the world of property. I checked out a number of people who were promoting themselves as 'experts' as I really wanted to work with somebody with absolute integrity who shoots from the heart but nonetheless is the best at what they do.

When I spent time with Glenn at the Berkshire property meeting in January 2011, he was that man. He just melted my brain in less than half an hour with the genius of his creativity and his absolute integrity. To this day, I have never seen anyone not progress under Glenn's care.

As I have heard Glenn say more than once, "You don't know what you don't know".

I could see that Glenn's business was larger than mine. I wanted to learn what he knew. I wanted to be in a cutting-edge environment where I could benefit from the synergy of working with knowledgeable people and move forward in the current market.

When you've been retired for four years, you can get quite comfortable and that had become a way of life, but now I was really ready to re-engage with the market and build even bigger than before.

The thing I really appreciated about Glenn is his creative mind. He can come up with ideas and strategies that are amazing. He is well ahead of his time. I also appreciate his seemingly endless energy and his tenacious commitment to help.

If you are looking to build a successful property business of your own, my advice would be to spend as much time as you can with him, do everything that he says, and you cannot go wrong.

"Take up one idea.
Make that one idea
your life –
think of it,
dream of it,
live on that idea.
Let the brain, muscles, nerves,
every part of your body,
be full of that idea,
and just leave every
other idea alone.

This is the way to success."

Swami Vivekananda

About the Author

I believe that there is a difference that makes the difference. If you want to earn more and achieve more than most other people, then you will have put in more effort than they do. You need to be that difference.

In life, the same opportunities are open to everyone – but not everyone sees them as opportunities, and those that do are rarely prepared to do what it takes to make them work. If you are action-orientated, have a vision about what you want to achieve, the willingness to learn and the drive to make things happen, then I can help you to do what I have done over the years.

As a property multi-millionaire myself, so far I have helped over 69 people become millionaires in their own right. Could you be the next?

I started out with nothing. I created my own opportunities by seeing things that others didn't. I worked very hard and eventually, at the age of 29, became a millionaire, in a non-property related business. Then I lost it all and was back to rock-bottom. However, I didn't let this setback destroy my confidence in myself or my vision. I started again and became a multi-millionaire again – by putting into practice what I had learned on my journey. This is what I will be sharing with you in this book.

I always say that the secret to success is having good judgement. In my workshops and training events, people ask me, "So where can I learn to have good judgement?" to which I reply, "Good judgement comes from experience." They then ask, "So where can I get experience?" You get experience from making poor judgements and making mistakes – and learning from them. Of course, another way to reduce your mistakes is to learn from a mentor and to learn from their experience.

If you are clever, you will learn something new from every experience you have had, both good and bad. I know that I have. I wish I could say that all my judgements have been good ones, but I would be fooling myself.

However, there was one question that I once asked that changed my life and unlocked the riches that I now have. Look out for that killer question as you read on!

For me, success is not about just following a formula or just having a proven strategy; it is equally about the sort of person you are, your values, and your mindset.

Many of us have been unhelpfully programmed by negative relatives or childhood experiences which can stand in the way of us achieving their full potential. That is why I shall also be focusing on mindset in this book.

I hope that my story and the things I have learned on my journey will inspire and help you to achieve even greater things. My wish for you is that, as a result, you will become my next Property Millionaire!

If that's what you want, start now! Read this book, take notes and, more importantly, take action! Procrastination is your greatest enemy.

"You must take
personal responsibility.
You cannot change
the circumstances,
the seasons, or the wind,
but you can change yourself.
That is something you have charge of."

Jim Rohn

*"You can have everything
in life you want,
if you will just help other people
get what they want."*

Zig Ziglar

How to become a
PROPERTY
MILLIONAIRE?

GLENN ARMSTRONG

LEARN THE SECRETS OF THE UK'S LEADING PROPERTY MILLIONAIRE MAKER

Published by
Filament Publishing Ltd
16 Croydon Road, Beddington, Croydon,
Surrey, CR0 4PA, United Kingdom.

Telephone +44(0)20 8688 2598
www.filamentpublishing.com

© 2018 Glenn Armstrong
ISBN 978-1-912635-20-7

Edited by Chris Day
Printed by 4Edge

The information contained within this book is strictly for
educational purposes. If you wish to apply ideas contained in
this book, you are taking full responsibility for your actions.

Table of Contents

*"A dream
becomes a goal
when action is taken
toward its achievement."*

Bo Bennett

Chapter One

What is your story?

We all have one. Our story is what we tell people to justify the fact that where we are today is not our fault, it was somebody else's. If it wasn't for them, for the economy, for the change in the market or whatever, we would now be successful. Oh yes! But before you tell your story again, and get those knowing nods and sympathetic words from the people around you, I have to tell you that this book is a No Excuse Zone. Please leave your story behind and leave your excuses in the cloakroom; this is not the place for them.

You probably don't want to hear this, but you are who you are, where you are and what you are as a result of all the hundreds and thousands of decisions you have taken over the years. Every time you chose the easy option, rather than the right option, every time you bottled it, every time you didn't do what your gut was telling you that you should, has brought you to this moment. Each decision builds on the previous one, and that is why you are here.

But here is the good news. The past is the past. There is no use looking back and saying, "If only..." It is too late! What you can change is your future. What happens from here on, you can do differently – if you choose to!

You are about to marry success

If you accept that you, and you alone, are in charge of what happens in your life, then you have taken the first step in moving forward.

It was Albert Einstein who said that "insanity is doing the same thing over and over again and expecting different results" and yet that is what we so often do. If you have ambitions to become a millionaire, which is perfectly possible, you will not achieve this by thinking in the same way that you have done in the past. Your present way of thinking has got you what you have now. If that is not enough, then it is time to change. Are you ready to make that change?

"Change is the law of life.
And those who look only
to the past or present
are certain to
miss the future."

John F. Kennedy

So, who are you?

I find that people take my one-day property event or join my Mentoring Programme from many walks of life. Some of them are already involved with property in one form or another. They may be estate agents or developers. They may be architects or specialists of one sort or another. Equally they may be just ordinary people who want to achieve something extra-ordinary and build a property portfolio in order to look after their retirement and loved ones. The point is, you do not need any previous experience in order to succeed – and there are not many opportunities with this potential that can say that.

You might not need experience, but you do need some very specific qualities.

- *You will need to be able to listen, study and learn*. You will be receiving a lot of information, strategies, case studies, legal frameworks, and the benefit of all my experience – and I don't hold back! You will need to be able to process and understand all the knowledge you will receive.

- *You need to have the ability to make decisions and follow through.*
  Opportunities can be lost if you spend too much time weighing up the pros and cons. Being a successful property entrepreneur doesn't happen unless you are able to move quickly. As you will learn from some of my case studies, speed can be of the essence in a dog-eat-dog world.

- ***You will need to have integrity.***
  You will be respected by your values. You will only succeed if people can trust you and rely on your word – especially when you are dealing with investors and private lenders. Your reputation needs to be spotless.

- ***You will need to be totally professional in everything you do.***
  If you want to be the person that others feel confident in doing business with, you will need to conduct your affairs in a consistent, timely, predictable and professional manner.

- ***You will need to project confidence and competence.***
  People need to feel that you are the right person to deal with.

- ***You need to have a positive mindset.***
  After all, you are a provider of solutions and positive outcomes. Never forget, attitudes are contagious – make sure yours is worth catching!

- ***You need to have a vision for your future.***
  You need to be goal centred, and determined to do what it takes to succeed. Would you do business with someone who didn't know where they were going?

- ***Finally, you need to have a clear 'why'.***
  You need to know why you are prepared to go down this road. What drives you? What is your motivation for getting out of bed? Why are you passionate about this? You need to know!

There will be times when things go wrong; after all, we all live in the real world and not everything goes according to plan. When it doesn't, you need to be able to remind yourself of why you are doing this in order to get back out there and continue. It is easy to lose heart and confidence when things go wrong. Always be able to anchor yourself with the reasons you set out on this journey, and you'll soon get back on track.

As you will read later on in the book, there have been multiple times when my world has fallen apart. In the space of one phone call, I lost £1 million. That hurt. It hurt a lot. However, I was able to pick myself up, dust myself down and start all over again. Your motivation, and what drives you, are what you will need to be able to do this yourself.

If you look through the curriculum of my courses, don't be put off by the amount of detail or the complexity of the subject. Yes, the journey to becoming a successful property investor and developer can be complicated at first and there is a lot to learn; however, you are not alone. When you read some of the positive comments that people have written having been on my courses, you will realise that you are a part of a very supportive community. You will make many new friends and useful contacts at our events, and you will find that everybody supports each other. We will always be there for you to help you achieve the big goals that you set for yourself.

*"Nothing in this world can
take the place of Persistence.
Talent will not:
nothing is more common than
unsuccessful men with talent.
Genius will not;
unrewarded genius
is almost a proverb.
Education will not:
the world is full of
educated derelicts.
Persistence and determination
alone are omnipotent."*

Calvin Coolidge

Chapter Two

My 'Why'

People often ask me what motivates me. Surely with a £45 million property portfolio, I don't need to be motivated, I can just sit back and enjoy the fruits of my labour. Far from it. Do I need to take time out of my life to spend four days at a time running my intensive property investment courses or spend time mentoring people? No, I don't need to, but I choose to, and this is why.

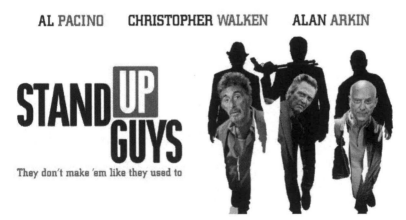

I once watched the film *Stand Up Guys*, which was released in 2012. It is an American crime-comedy, directed by Fisher Stevens and starring Al Pacino, Christopher Walken and Alan Arkin. *Stand Up Guy* is an American phrase meaning a loyal and reliable friend.

In the film, Al Pacino says the following:

"They say we die twice. Once when the last breath leaves our body and once when the last person we knew, says our name for the last time.
Then our life will be forgotten."

My 'Why' is that I want to leave a lasting legacy. Something that will live on. I want to make a difference in people's lives for the better, and I want to leave something for my family to live on.

With my intensive property courses and my Mentoring Programme, what gives me the greatest satisfaction is watching people put in to practice what they have learned, and go on to repeat the same success that I have enjoyed, and for them to build a successful business of their own and become millionaires in their own right.

So far I have helped at least 69 people achieve that goal. What better satisfaction and fulfilment could I possibly have?

The Looks on their Faces
by Glenn Armstrong

For the looks on their faces is why I do this, you know,
The old and the young show so much joy when they achieve
a goal they have set.

❧

For the looks on their faces is why I do this, you know,
To help them and make sure a better life they can get
Their pension a concern but never yet

❧

For the looks on their faces is why I do this, you know,
The striving forward to the goal is more rewarding
when putting the effort and learned skills into achieving it.
Something we work hard at then succeed
is far more rewarding than being handed it, I believe.

❧

For the looks on their faces is why I do this, you know,
Before you know it, tomorrow will become today.
You need to work, not just hard but smart, so you can play.

❧

For the looks on their faces is why I do this, you know,
Onward and upward, we persist,
never giving upon our dream to exist
in a more comfortable life with choices,
I love hearing the hope in their voices,
especially when I have just shown them how.

❧

For the looks on their faces is why I do this, you know,
There is nothing I like better than having someone who I helped come
up and shake my hand and say "thank you,
you have changed my life and my family's life forever".
For the looks on their faces is why I do this, you know.

"The pessimist sees difficulty in every opportunity. The optimist sees the opportunity in every difficulty."

Winston Churchill

Chapter Three
The start of my entrepreneurial journey

As I said at the beginning, everyone has a story, but it is how you use it that counts. You can use your old story as an excuse, or you can use it to inspire others to do what you have done – and make changes in their lives.

When you are busy living your life and working in the real world, you sometimes don't realise the significance of some of the things that happened to you or what you learned from them. Growing up as a youngster, it never occurred to me that many of my experiences were training me to be an entrepreneur. In fact, I couldn't even spell the word, let alone know what it meant.

One clue was at the age of five when my mum asked me what I wanted to be when I grew up. My instinctive answer was that I wanted to be Father Christmas. "Why?" she asked. "Because I'll only have to work one day in the year!" Obviously I didn't have a nine-to-five job in mind even then!

That is not to say I was work-shy. Far from it, but I was always on the lookout for opportunities to earn money and being work smart!

One of my first ventures at the age of ten was to go to the houses of my friends and ask their mums if they had any unwanted toys. Nine times out of ten, they did, and they were happy to give them to me. It was too good an opportunity! I set up little jumble sales to raise money for the Boys Brigade at our church. It was a great success.

Free stock and no overheads? That is a good lesson to learn while still at primary school.

Even at this early age, I was already very alert to opportunities to make money. Needless to say, I was already buying packets of sweets, repackaging them into smaller quantities, and selling them to my school chums at a profit.

If you give people what they want,
they'll always be pleased to pay for it.
That lesson still works for me today!

Did you sell and make money from sweets to your chums at school? If so, it may well be a pointer to the fact that you too have entrepreneurial genes! A great gift to have.

Like other kids, I also had a paper round. I didn't mind getting up early if there was money to earn. My brother also wanted to do the same but was too young to be doing it, so I would collect the papers from the shop for him to deliver and paid him a wage from my earnings. After all, business is business, family or not!

Just round the corner from where I lived, there were a couple of boys that I knew. They had told me that their mother paid them a penny to do household tasks like the washing-up or mowing the lawn, so when I persuaded a leaflet distribution company to let me deliver a number of different leaflets to 1,000 local houses for them, I immediately knew who I was going to call!

I was paid £16 for every 1,000 leaflets I delivered, so I called on my two friends to help me. I would pay them a pound to deliver the same amount. For them, this was a 100% increase in their earnings from their mum and they jumped at it. The arrangement worked very well, until one of them got to hear what I was being paid. This resulted in a visit from their mum to my mum. The lesson I learned from that was,

Keep your business affairs to yourself;
don't tell people what you are earning,
and don't gossip!

Of course, some times of the year are more expensive than others so, with Christmas looming, I had to devise some new ways to make money. As it was November, I thought we would try the 'penny for the Guy'. We started with a normal Guy dressed up with clothes we found around the house. We did alright but then we hit on the idea of dressing my brother us as the Guy – and we made even more money. Another lesson to be learned there!

When Christmas got closer, I had my eye on a very impressive blue racing bike. It cost £20 – a small fortune. I hoped that Santa would bring it to me on Christmas Eve. Of course, I dropped very broad hints to that effect, but my mum had other ideas.

She gave me £5 towards it and my nan gave me another £5. I was told the rest was down to me. Now there was an incentive! But what to do? I came up with the idea of carol singing. This was a great plan with the minor exception that I didn't know any carols and couldn't sing! But that didn't deter me. I got my friends together who could sing and did know some carols. I just stood at the back and mimed! My three-year-old sister was given the collecting tin to hold!

"You don't have to be good at everything yourself, as long as you know people who are."

People started to ask us if the money was going to charity and that made me think, so we started to donate a percentage of our earnings to the Boys Brigade at the church. They gave us a certificate to confirm we have made the donation which we then displayed – and the donations flooded in. I put some of it towards the charity and the rest towards my bike. There is no greater feeling than earning money to enable you to buy what you want. To this day, my dad still has this bike in his garage.

But there was something else that happened that Christmas that had a profound impact on me.

Do you remember the iconic 1951 film of Charles Dickens' *A Christmas Carol* with Alastair Sim as Ebenezer Scrooge? There was Scrooge sitting in his freezing office on Christmas Eve with his staff pleading with him to put another piece of coal on the fire. I remember it well.

It was close to Christmas and my mum asked me to go with her to check on Mrs Schweitzer, an elderly lady that lived next door to us. It just so happened that the weather was horrible – high winds and snow. Even though we were just walking next door, we had to wrap up well against the weather.

Mum let us in with her key, as she often visited our neighbour to make sure she was alright. The house was freezing and I kept my coat on. There in the front room was the lady sitting in her armchair with a blanket over her legs and a shawl on. In front of her was a single bar of an electric fire. I was horrified that somebody should be living in this terrible way. I offered to switch on the other bar of the fire to warm the room up.

"No," she said, "I can only afford to have one bar on." This upset me. Nobody should have to live this way in a freezing cold house. I was determined to do something about it.

When the spring came, I offered to clear and cultivate her garden. I grew all sorts of vegetables. When they were ready, I went round to all of our friends' parents and sold all our homegrown produce cheaper than they could buy them in the shops. With the income that I made, I shared it with our neighbour to help pay her electricity bill so her house could be warmer in the winter.

To this day, I have a phobia about a cold house. If we are ever away, I will always leave the heating on so it is warm when we return.

Our neighbour is long passed away now but her memory stays with me and the important lesson that I learned from her.

"The purpose
of human life
is to serve,
and to show
compassion
and the will
to help others."

Albert Schweitzer

Chapter Four

Finding my way

We all have to discover who we are and where our strengths lie, but sometimes this takes a little trial and error before we hit on what our destiny is going to be. Having discovered at an early age that I had an aptitude for business, I wondered what I could do once I left school.

My first job introduced me to the world of retail. There was a position advertised at a local branch of Shoppers Paradise, the discount grocery chain that was a part of the Fine Fare group. It was one of those 'pile it high and sell it cheap' stores. No fancy displays, just piles of cardboard boxes with the front cut out. This was the time before barcodes, scanners and intelligent tills. We didn't even have price tickets. Our job was to remember the prices and punch them into old-fashioned tills. I had to develop a great memory very quickly. Due to this, they did pay well. I was earning a whole £42 a week, which might not sound much today but went a very long way then, aged 18 and living with parents.

Working in retail and sales puts you at the sharp end of working with customers and learning communication skills. It was a pressured environment and they worked us hard. Whilst it wasn't going to be a long-term career, it did teach me some invaluable skill sets.

It was my father that had bigger dreams for me and pointed out that I was in a dead-end job. If I was to make anything of myself,

I would need to get an apprenticeship and a traditional job that had prospects. It was difficult to fault his logic.

I applied for a job at Marconi Avionics, then a part of the GEC group. I was successful and started training to become a trainee mechanical design engineer. A big change! I was just 19.

Now I was part of a huge organisation with a job that had prospects. I looked around me and saw many employees that had been there the whole of their working lives. Could this be my future? I wasn't sure, but I knuckled down and put all of my energy into making a success of my tasks and goals.

Of course, I had taken a pay cut to do this at my father's request. My income had dropped from £42 per week to a miserly £18.

Around that time, in 1980, I fell in love with a local girl in Hatfield where I was living at the time. Her parents moved Milton Keynes, which was a new town in a development area. I learned from them that GEC was opening a new division there and were looking for staff. Not only that but, as an incentive for people to move there to work, they were being offered a house by the development corporation. What a great opportunity! They offered us a two-bedroom house, but I managed to persuade them to give us a three-bedroom house. This was to become a valuable asset later with the Right to Buy scheme.

I successfully applied to move to the new plant and was offered a three-bedroom house close by. When I shared the news with my girlfriend's parents, it was made very clear to me that we could not move in together without getting married. As her father was an ex-Grenadier Guards boxing champion, I knew that any negotiations on the subject would be futile. So within the space of one week, I moved jobs, moved house and got married. Quite eventful!

I started working locally and quickly settled in to the new plant. It wasn't long before a new opportunity arrived. Although I didn't realise it then, it was going to be instrumental in my becoming a millionaire for the first time, and it all started with something tiny and insignificant, as all the best opportunities do.

"Sometimes
opportunities
float right
past your nose.
Work hard,
apply yourself,
and be ready.
When an opportunity comes
you can grab it."

Julie Andrews

Chapter Five

From a tiny acorn...

Looking back, I can now see how my experiences in my early years contributed to my entrepreneurial mindset. All those microbusinesses, the growing and selling vegetable to my friends' parents, the carol singing, penny for the Guy and the toy sales, all gave me a grounding in the principle that, if you give people what they want, they are pleased to give you money in return. I could not have learned a better lesson. So what happened next?

A neighbour was emigrating abroad and needed to dispose of all the things he couldn't take with him. One of these items was a video recorder and 11 films on VHS. Today that doesn't sound like a big deal, but back then, long before videos could be streamed, long before DVDs and all of the high-tech gadgets we are used to today, a video recorder was quite expensive and not many people had one. Back then, they were a bit of a novelty.

I agreed to buy the recorder and the films from him. As it turned out, this was one of the best purchases I have ever made. Naturally, my colleagues back in the works got to hear that I had it and asked if they could hire it overnight to watch a film. I agreed.

"How much do you want?" they asked. I came up with a figure. Before very long, the video player and a film were being rented out every night, and I was struggling to keep up with demand.

When WH Smith had a sale, I increased my list to 35 films, giving people a real choice. Titles such as *The Deer Hunter* and *One Flew Over the Cuckoo's Nest* were very popular. The girls in the office agreed to type up my list and run some copies in the print room for me to take round the works. A new business was being born and I called it Wunday Videos – as people were renting the video machine for just 'one day'.

I spent my time going round the whole works site with my list and taking orders to rent out the video machine. My boss turned a blind eye to my activities, mainly because I would let him use the machine once a week for free.

I now needed to expand so I approached a local electrical store who agreed to rent me another video machine for £16 per month. As I was renting them out at £4 per night, I was well in profit Overnight, I was able to double my turnover! In today's terms, I suppose I was renting to rent!

I was on to a winner, so I kept on buying new films and increasing the number of machines I could rent out. My next step was to start dropping leaflets in to houses local to where I lived and increasing my customer base.

This continued for a while. I was earning a salary as an apprentice in Marconi which was now £100 per week. On a Saturday, I was earning £40 per week playing for the local football team, and in my spare time I was earning £400 per week renting our videos and machines. This probably made me the highest paid person in the Marconi plant! But I was really working hard.

I would start work at 6 a.m. and do three hours' overtime. I would get home at 5 p.m. and start my video round, getting home from that at 9 p.m. I would then do my homework and study for my exams.

On a Tuesday and Thursday evening, I would go to football practice in the evening. On a Saturday, I would work another three hours overtime in the morning, play football for the club in the afternoon and do my video round in the evening.

One Saturday, I was walking back from football past my local Jaguar garage and I saw a car which, amazingly, had my name on it! The number plate was GLN 86T. It had 'Glenn' on it, which was good enough for me. It wasn't a Jaguar but a very sexy Ford Capri RS 3.1 with full racing spec. It was the dog's wobbly bits and it was on sale for £3,500. The moment was right; I had to have it! I suppose this was the start of my fascination with fast cars which, as you will discover, has lasted a long time.

I drove the Capri in to work and, believe me, it turned heads. Pulling in behind me was my boss driving his pride and joy – a Toyota Celica. He saw my car and that was it! He stopped me doing the videos – dead! He did not like me having a better car than him.

As it happened, a few weeks later the results of my mechanical design engineer's exam came through and the head of my section invited me in to his office to give me the results and to offer me an increase in salary and a move to a new department. At the time, I was working on guided missiles so it really was rocket science. In my five years there, my wages had grown to £100 per week and I was about to be offered double.

However, I surprised him by saying, "Do you know what? I am going to hand in my notice."

I could not see my future working nine-to-five for somebody else when I already knew I could make vastly more working for myself.

Unfortunately the casualty of all my hard work and long hours was my marriage. There is no question that with my focus on building my business in the evening, working full-time during the day, playing for the football club at weekends and studying the rest of the time, it meant it didn't leave much quality time. My work-life balance was well out of balance, and unfortunately that cost me my marriage.

I was now 23 and had left the security of what would then have been a job for life, complete with a pension, to work for myself, and I have never looked back. It was to be the last proper job I would ever have. I was single again and looking forward to the next chapter in my life.

"There's no such thing as work-life balance. There are work-life choices, and you make them, and they have consequences."

Jack Welch

Chapter Six

Moving into the big time

By this time, the video business was really motoring. I had six agents working for me now and six separate rounds going out every day around the area. The leaflet distribution was really paying off.

This meant I had a stream of cars coming to my house at 6 p.m. every day to collect the cases of videos we had prepared for them, and the same again at 9 p.m. when they returned. Once everything had been accounted for, I would go out nightclubbing until 2 a.m. The following morning, I would sleep in until 10 a.m. when I would have somebody come in to prepare the cases of videos for the rounds that night. We had a good routine going. Maybe too good.

We were starting to make a bit of an impact in the street, and it wasn't long before we had a knock at the door from the council telling us that we couldn't run a business from the house. I suppose it was inevitable, but it was also a catalyst in helping us to look at a new way to grow the business. We needed a shop!

I was mindful that this would be an overhead we hadn't had before so I didn't want to spend too much. I noticed that there was a small launderette not too far away that was unoccupied. It would be perfect! The downside was that it was £25 per week.

But, as they say, you don't know what you don't know, so I took it on. We fitted out the shop as best we could with items left from the previous tenants. This included welding up the back door and window to make sure we were not broken into. It wasn't the best of areas. However, that turned out to be to our advantage. On our first day, we turned over £200. I was amazed!

We had not put any thought to the type of people that rented videos. We found out very quickly that the area we had chosen for our shop could not have been better. It was a low-income area where people would rent a video for a good night in, rather than spending money they didn't have for a night out. A lucky coincidence! But there was a downside.

Our business model had changed. Instead of having agents go to our clients' houses to deliver and collect the videos, our clients were now visiting us in the shop – and some of them didn't have good memories because they forgot to bring the videos back. This was a problem.

"Ever since I was a child I have had this instinctive urge for expansion and growth. To me, the function and duty of a quality human being is the sincere and honest development of one's potential."

Bruce Lee

But with every problem, there is also a solution. I heard about a local man who was tall and quite muscular. He had been drinking outside a local pub when he had been set upon by a local gang of seven. He floored them all to the delight of the other customers, and, for some reason, was never bothered again. However, news of what happened reached me and I tracked him down.

"How would you like to get all of your videos for free?" I asked him.

"What's the catch?" he asked in return.

"All I need you to do is to collect overdue videos from local customers."

"Oh, I can do that," he said. I now had a collector! To help, we also took a picture of our customers when they rented a video so he knew who to look for. You can run, but you can't hide! The problem of the stolen videos was now resolved.

I put his picture in the window with the message that, if you forgot to bring your video back, we would come and collect it – and there would be a fine. It did the trick. My customers miraculously regained their memories! Problem solved.

We soon realised that we now had a winning formula. The shop was now well-established and a success. There was only one thing to do – expand by repeating the formula somewhere else. We looked for another shop in a similar area, found it and started over again. The empire was growing.

My first experience with property

I would love to say that my introduction to the world of property was as a result of research, a strategy and a plan, but the truth is that it was an accident. In fact, worse than that; it was an impulse. A friend asked me to accompany him to a property auction as he wanted to buy a house and needed some moral support. As it happened, he didn't buy the one he was looking for because it went for more than he could afford, but towards the end of the sale, when most people had spent their money, the auctioneer was offering a two-bedroom house in Netherfield for just £12,000. For me, that seemed very cheap. On impulse, I raised my hand and bought it. I had done no due diligence, I didn't know the property, but I was lucky. When I visited the house, it was actually alright.

I got a friend to cut the grass, and give it a lick of paint throughout. I put down a second-hand carpet and then put an advert in the video shop window to sell it for £22,000. It sold in three days. What the property was actually worth, I don't know to this day. Whether I sold it too cheaply or not, I have no idea, but I had learned something important. Why didn't I do it again?

By this time, my empire had grown to five video shops and I had plans to take it up to 15.

"Real estate investing, even on a very small scale, remains a tried and true means of building an individual's cash flow and wealth."

Robert Kiyosaki

Despite my focus being on the shops, properties kept coming along just begging to be bought. I was able to buy my council house and also the council house belonging to the new girlfriend I was with at the time. An estate agent I knew called me up to alert me to a property that had come on to the market that day and that was a real bargain. Did I want it? I said yes and put a deposit down without a second thought. Big mistake!

What I should have done is discussed it with my girlfriend. It was indeed a good bargain, a nice four-bedroom house in Willen, but when I took her round it, all I got was, "I don't like it, I don't like it,"– all because I bought it without her. Another life lesson learned!

Fortunately a nice detached five-bedroom house came up for £160,000 off-plan, which she did like, so I bought that as well.

The plans for expanding the video store business were calling for capital so I spoke to the bank about funding but all I got was, 'The computer says no!' So it was Plan B. I sold the first house in Willen. I had bought it for £108,000 and sold it 12 weeks later for £140,000. Not a bad turnaround, and the profit went into expanding the shop chain.

Before long, the number of shops had grown to 15. By now, I was just 29 years old with a very successful business and we had caught the attention of a national chain, Video Store plc, a part of the Binatone Group. They offered me £1.5 million for the business and I accepted. I took enough in cash to pay off my debts and the rest I took in shares, so on paper at any rate, I was now a millionaire. I had come a long way from Shoppers Paradise.

Chapter Seven

From hero to zero

So what do people do when they become millionaires? Well in my case, go out every night with friends, party and have a good time. Yes, I had the five-bedroom house now, but I was single again. Not clever.

Hindsight is always 20:20 vision

Two wasted years later, I read in the paper the fact that Video Store plc had gone bust. All my £1 million worth of shares that I had left in the company were now worthless. Other than a few grand in the bank, I was back to square one. A real wake-up call. What on earth was I going to do now? Playtime was well and truly over!

Personal development

It wasn't until the crash of the video shops and my going from millionaire to zero in a matter of minutes, that I really became interested in personal development. When you get to rock bottom, as I had, you need to have a good personal philosophy to get you through it and out the other side. Opportunity is no use to you if your head is not right. You either won't recognise it or you will make a mess of it by focusing on the wrong things.

I was with a new girlfriend now who was less than pleased with our new change of circumstances. I thought back to my previous successes and what I had done to become a millionaire in the first place. I reckoned that if I could do it once, I could do it again. All I needed was the right vehicle. So what would it be this time?

With the video stores, I had hit the market at exactly the right time. The technology was right, the route to market was right, and the demand was there. But the writing was on the wall and I could see new technology about to make sweeping changes.

Kissing frogs

I embarked on a search to find the next big success. I had total confidence in myself and my abilities, but what I needed was a little bit of luck as well. My initial criteria was to find something that could generate around £3,000 per week for me with the potential to be scalable so I could grow it as I did before.

I started to try too hard. I started with a print shop, printing mugs and T-shirts. I tried selling cars but I wasn't getting close to my target of earning £3,000 per week and I had yet to see anything that had to potential to explode in the same way that the video business had.

We were starting to get low on money and my girlfriend was getting frustrated with me. Her solution? For me to get a job. I wouldn't hear of it! Once you've been a millionaire, you don't go back to work in Tesco! We had a blazing row and I put my fist through a door – something I had never done before, or since.

Unfortunately, she was right. If I kept on doing what I was doing, we would keep on earning what we were earning, and that wasn't enough. So we compromised and I started driving a cab.

If you have never driven a cab, let me tell you, it is soul-destroying. Trust me! It is not as if everything you earn goes into your pocket. Oh no! You have to pay your radio rent, your petrol, your private hire insurance, and still pay for your car. The reality is that your first few hours go towards paying for all that before you earn a penny.

It was interesting to watch how my fellow drivers were doing. Most of them gave themselves a target of what they wanted to earn each day. Once they hit their target, they stopped working. So incredibly, if it was raining, which is always a busy time for cabs, they would still stop when they hit their target. That made no sense to me. Their mindset seemed to be about living for today. That wasn't for me. All this time I was learning about how this industry worked and if there were some opportunities to be had. There were. But not behind the wheel.

The first car I used, I had to rent. It cost £80 per week. It seemed that most other drivers did the same thing. I also learned that many of the drivers had bad credit and couldn't buy a car in the usual way. Driving a minicab seemed what you did when you couldn't do anything else. So I thought, how can I reinvent this?

Suppose I were to buy a car for £3,000 and offer it for hire to them at £125 per week. That was more than they were paying but suppose that at the end of the two years, they could buy it off me for £1? Now that was different!

How could I make this possible? I didn't have £3,000! But what I did have was time and determination. I worked out that to earn £3,000, I needed to work an extra ten hours a week. That would make an extra £100 a week, so in 30 weeks, I could buy a car. I had to work 50 hours in order to pay my bills. If I worked an extra ten hours, it would give me an extra £100 which would then take me 30 weeks to buy a car. I had to go through the 50 hours of pain before I got to the ten hours of gain.

I decided that, to speed this up, in addition to the 50 hours I needed, I would work an additional 30 hours and get to the £3,000 three times as quick. This meant I could look forward to 20 weeks when I didn't have to do the 50 hours. It was a plan – and it worked! The interesting thing was that none of the other drivers were doing this – they just stopped working when they had earned enough for that day.

However, there was a problem. I was impatient and I was hungry for my next success. So instead of working a little bit more and taking 30 weeks, I worked really hard and did it in ten weeks. I now had my first car to rent out. My next car only took eight weeks. I ended up with a fleet of 30 cabs rented out at £125 per week. On average, I was making £100 per week per taxi. I had cracked it! My target of earning £3,000 per month had been reached. I stopped driving and had somebody collect the money for me. Job done! Or was it?

"Everyone is an entrepreneur.
The only skills you need
to be an entrepreneur:
an ability to fail,
an ability to have ideas,
to sell those ideas,
to execute on those ideas,
and to be persistent
so even as you fail
you learn
and move onto the next adventure."

James Altucher

Chapter Eight

The next adventure

The trouble with being an entrepreneur is that the job is never done. Once you have created a new business and grown it to a point where it is self-sufficient and generating a profit, there is an urge to look for the next challenge. I read about a guy called Dillon, who was recognised by the Prince's Trust as their Young Entrepreneur of the Year for his business, a computer games mail order company. Mail order? Computer games? This was a market I had not thought about before. Maybe this could be the next big thing? I set about to research how it worked, where the opportunities might be and where the games were manufactured.

With mail order, I quickly found that it all hinged on being able to process credit cards from people that have written to you with an order for stock. Naturally I approached the bank to set up this facility, only to find that banks consider mail order to be risky. Their concern centred around returns, refunds, non-delivery, stolen cards, and a list of other challenges I'd never thought of. I had hit a brick wall.

Not one to take no for an answer, I took my request higher within the bank until I found someone to say, "Yes." However, it was a "Yes, but..." They wanted me to come up with a bond of £6,000 as a safety net just in case it went wrong. Not helpful!

In the meantime, I had been sourcing games manufacturers and looking into the dynamics of the games marketplace. I started by buying a few hundred popular games here and there, and selling them by advertising and through games wholesalers who distributed them to the proliferation of small computer games shops that had sprung up around the country. I quickly discovered that the money was in wholesaling rather than retailing. Even though we only had a margin of around 50p a game, when you are bulk selling to wholesalers, it soon added up. The games we sold direct to consumers were generating a profit of around £15 to £20 each.

By chance, I met with somebody who was friends with the managing director of Sony in Turkey. As a result of that connection, we started importing games by the lorry-load and selling to the wholesalers. As we were able to go back to the source, we now had a far better margin and were making at least £4 per game. Incredibly, within three years our turnover grew to £12 million. Maybe this was the next big thing?

Games such as *Spyro the Dragon* and *Crash Bandicoot* became huge sellers as computer gaming really took off. Things were doing well, but then we started to notice that a lot of the little shops we were supplying to were starting to close. What was happening? We soon discovered that Tesco had muscled into the market and were selling the games at a discount in their stores. The bubble had burst. It had just been a fad. It was time to move on and start again, but what on earth should we do next? To answer that, I was about the ask the most important question of my life.

Chapter Nine

The multi-million pound question

As you know, my lifelong passion has been for cars. Today I have a stable of them, including a Bentley Continental Supersports convertible, an Aston Martin DB9 convertible, a Rolls-Royce Ghost and a Ferrari 458 Spider, but back then I was just window shopping.

I was talking to a friend of mine who had a garage selling Ferraris and Lamborghinis. I asked him what was to be the most important question of my life so far. I said, "What sort of people buy cars like this?" What I was really saying was, "So who are the people with the money?"

He answered, "40% of my customers are in IT, and 40% are in property." My ears pricked up. Property? I know a bit about that from the past. Maybe this could be the big one?

Then *The Sunday Times Rich List* came out, and sure enough 50% of the people on the list had made their money through property. That clinched it. Property it was going to be. So in 2004, I set up my property company and have never looked back.

We dived into property without any great strategy and working on instinct rather than knowledge. In a short period of time, we had purchased, at a very good price, a total of six properties before we ran out of money. We needed a plan and we needed to get it right. All I knew is that we needed to buy properties cheaply enough to be able to refinance them further down the line and get our money out.

We looked at how we could work with solicitors, and how we could streamline our relationship with building societies so we could get finance and refinance quickly. We needed to put this onto a professional footing, and create a production line.

Big plans

We set ourselves the goal of buying a property a week, and in the next 12 months we actually achieved 52 properties in 48 weeks. We now had well over 100 properties with an amazing cash flow and a very low loan to value – and they are appreciating all the time!

"No matter what the government does,
no matter what is happening
in the marketplace,
no matter what the economy is doing,
you can always make money in property –
if you know what you are doing
and have the right strategy."

Glenn Armstrong

By now, we did know what we were doing. We had good relationships in place with all of the professionals and organisations we needed, and we had a track record and a good reputation locally as ethical landlords and a safe pair of hands in the marketplace. This was vital in our ability to grow.

Our challenge was getting properties at the right prices. We soon learned that estate agents were not the best place to achieve this. Their focus is on how much they can sell them for, not how little! We needed a different source.

I thought back to the time when I was buying and selling cars. If you wanted to retail a car at a profit, you wouldn't buy it from a dealer in the first place. A main dealer needs to make a profit himself so is never going to give you the best of prices. Back then, I would advertise in local newspapers 'Cars bought for cash'. This way, you could get a good price and make a profit.

Would the same principle work for property? I had to find out!

I started to put adverts in the local press to test the market and almost immediately got enquiries. I discovered that there were people who had to sell, and quickly as their finances were in a mess and repossession beckoned. They were only too grateful to have someone come along with a solution. What we could offer was speed and immediate cash. We were also getting the properties at very good prices, which fitted our business model. A gap in the market! Here we go again!

Not only were we learning as we went along, but we were always coming up with obstacles and challenges. I have always been creative and love finding innovative solutions to any problem.

I started putting my mind to those things that were holding us back.

We didn't look to copy what others were doing in the market, but rather invent our own strategies and solutions. We have continued this philosophy up to the present to the extent that many of the things we now implement and train are unique to us.

Today we are even advising solicitors on how to structure deals for their clients. There's nothing I like best than to charge a solicitor £1,000 an hour for my advice – and make them wait! Sweet justice!

As we move forward, we are now moving in to creating our own developments and opening up a range of new opportunities. But none of this would have happened if I had not asked that one question in the first place that started me thinking. It was indeed a multi-million pound question because that is precisely what it was created.

"There is no security
on this earth;
there is only
opportunity."

Douglas MacArthur

Chapter Ten

Taking action

At the beginning of my property career, I started buying properties and advertising in the local papers. Buying below market value, I got to a point where I had done ten deals in ten weeks. I was talking about it to someone and, as a result, I was asked to speak at an event that they were holding.

At that time, I had been doing property for only about a year but I had not really done any public speaking. Like most people, I was terrified at the thought of standing up in public to talk. It was well outside my comfort zone.

I wrote out my speech word for word on the subject of 'How I bought ten properties in ten weeks'. When I arrived on the day, there were 110 people in the room, a lot more than I was expecting. I hardly dared to look at them so I kept my head down and simply read out my notes. About ten minutes into my speech, I had a thought that I might be boring them so I glanced up to see if anyone was still there. To my surprise, they were, and sitting on the edge of their seats with their mouths open and listening attentively to my every word. They all wanted to know how I had done it.

At the end of the talk, I was surrounded with people asking questions. One lady asked if I did mentoring. "Of course," I said, thinking on my feet. "One thousand pounds a year." I had two take-ups right away. My mentoring business had started.

Due to the amount of interest in what I was doing and the number of question I was being asked, I decided to hold a free one-day training event. The deal was that they would give me feedback and/or a testimonial. The feedback was universally positive and, more importantly, they would be prepared to pay good money to attend future events. My training business had now started.

Based on their feedback, at my next event I charged £100 a ticket and easily filled the room. With more great testimonials and feedback, I had the courage to put the following event up to £300. I was still buying one property a week and everyone wanted to learn how.

Working closely with my attendees, I also realised that knowledge about property and strategies was not enough to ensure success. The attitude and mindsets of every individual also played a huge part in their future. I was going to have to be able to train this as well.

I started to work on those skills by learning about NLP, body language, negotiating skills, financial literacy, and all aspect of personal development to enable me to really influence their success.

My research into these subject brought me into contact with some of the most powerful books on success fundamentals ever written, authors like Dale Carnegie, Rhonda Byrne, Napoleon Hill, Zig Ziglar, Robert Kiyosaki, Stephen R. Covey, George Samuel Clason, Donald Trump, Norman Vincent Peale, Susan Jeffers, Desmond Morris and Dr Robert Cialdini. I have shared the key learning points I took from them later in the book.

Succeeding in the world of property is a lot more than strategies and formulae. You need to work as hard on yourself, your mindset, and your personal development as you do on your business. However, there is one caveat.

All too often, I have seen people put off starting the first steps of their property business, until they have 'all the information'. They see my recommended reading list and believe they should read it all before they get started. Wrong!

Read these books as your bedtime reading, when you are travelling on the train – or even when sitting in the smallest room in the house. Listen to CDs whilst you are driving. Every moment of your time is precious – use it well.

If you are getting ready to get ready, you are procrastinating and are using this as an excuse not to take action. It is what you <u>do</u> that will determine your success far more than what you know. When I first started, I didn't know what I didn't know and as a result, I made mistakes. But I was a fast learner and never slow to ask questions.

By working with someone who has done it before and has a track record of success, you can tap in to my experience as a property mentor and know that we will keep you on track. You are not on your own!

Now that my training and mentoring programmes were in place, it was the time to share what I had learned.

***There are people out there for whom the time is right,
right now, to make a dramatic change in their lives,
and to unleash their full potential.
Are you one of them?***

We have people approaching us who want to be able to give up their day job and build a business of their own. They are fed up with there being too much month at the end of the money and want to be in charge of their own future – something you can never be when you are working for someone else. The people who do well on our courses are those that have a burning desire to become financially free through building and managing a property portfolio – as soon as possible! Around 80% of our attendees fit that description. The remainder are professionals of one sort or another in the property industry.

I am honest with them and say, if you have got what it takes and really want to become a property millionaire, I can help you achieve it. Those are not just idle words, we have created at least 69 millionaires at the last count. I think it is actually more.

Probably the biggest thing I can offer is that I have made more mistakes than they have – but only once! If you are hungry for success, there just isn't enough time for you to make all those mistakes again yourself. Learn from mine!

People outside the world of property look at the swings in the marketplace, they look at the economy going up and down, they look at Brexit and the aftermath of that, they look at government flexing its muscles with legislation, and they see a minefield. How can they possibly navigate their way through?

But there is a way. In fact, there are multiple ways. You just need to learn what they are, and that's what we teach.

For example, the late Duke of Westminster would buy in recessions and do nothing in the booms. My preference is to develop during the booms and build up my portfolio in the busts. You need to arrive at your own strategy and what works for you.

My original portfolio was built up over three and a half years. The recession then came along, and when that happens the lenders get twitchy. In their eyes, we had too many properties so they chose not to lend to us. But there is always a way! As you know, I just love finding an innovative way around any problem. So what we started to do was to buy for other people.

We also came up with the strategy of breaking a house into rooms and selling the rooms. We also found a way of getting express refinance – same day! That helped to make a lot of things possible that would otherwise not have been.

For example, we found a property that was valued at £140,000, based on the fact that we wanted to refinance it even though we didn't own it, and we were able to apply for a remortgage on the property at its value of £140,000 (providing the value was confirmed by a surveyor).

We were getting 85% of that which was £119,000, so we were then able to buy the property in the morning for £100,000 which was the agreed price, and refinance it for £119,000 on the same day. The solicitors would then ask us where we would like them to send the difference, after costs.

Ever since we started our monthly intensive four-day property seminars, we have been oversubscribed. We normally have between 20 and 30 people in the room, and I share all my experience, strategies and processes. I don't hold anything back. Indeed, if you were to take everything that I share with you, plus all the printed notes, you will have everything you need to repeat what I have done.

Despite the fact that the monthly four-day event is hard work for me, I must admit that I get great satisfaction from seeing people's eyes open when they realise that this is something they can do – and indeed thrive at. Of course, it is not for everybody, but at the end of those four days, you will know if you have what it takes to make it as a successful property investor.

However, one of the things that is unique to my courses is the fact that we weave together mindset training with practical strategies. You need both. One without the other is no use. At one point in my life, I became an NLP master practitioner and this has been invaluable. It has help me when negotiating, when looking for people to work with, but most of all in helping people to overcome the obstacles that they have erected, which can jeopardise their success.

Some people I have met have worked incredibly hard in their lives, but never seem to have enjoyed the level of success they deserved. In talking to them and listening to what they had to say, I can very often pinpoint what that one thing is which is holding them back. This can sometimes mean tears, but for anyone who wants to make the rest of their life more successful than they have been up to this moment, it's a small price to pay.

For people who want to move faster and work closer with me, I have started a mentoring programme. Property courses can be a great way of accelerating your knowledge and success. However, after a course, how often do you get home, full of good intentions, only to lose your momentum after the first or second month – or, if the truth be known, even earlier?

To help you stay focused, my mentorship programme provides ongoing training and support with weekly daytime webinars and monthly mastermind days.

The mentorship programme offers a combination of education, brainstorming, peer accountability and support in a group setting to sharpen your business and personal skills. The group helps you and the rest of its members achieve success.

At each session, you will develop your personal business plan, set goals and objectives, and monitor and discuss problems, obstacles and successes that all the individuals within the group face. You will then review your previous month's goals and achievements.

We carry out negotiation exercises, building and improving your knowledge and skill set every month. As well as having guest speakers, who bring additional information and qualities to enhance your learning, I will personally go through deals that you're currently working on and see if there is potential to increase the returns.

I hold the monthly meetings in our offices and elsewhere, and you will also have access to my weekly two-hour interactive daytime webinars, where I will go through any deals you have or stumbling blocks you are currently facing or having trouble with.

Don't worry if you can't always make the live webinars; we record them so you can listen again for anything you missed. If you have questions and you aren't able to listen live, just email my team with your questions and I will answers these first to save you from having to listen to the full recording to hear your advice.

You can ask questions and gain knowledge from others who have already done what you are thinking about doing. All of our members are happy to share their knowledge and experience with you. There are several of their stories in this book.

Many people ask why my training mentorship programme is so much better value than other property education providers. The simple reason is this. My focus is on making money through property deals, not training. I love sharing what I know and helping people to do what I have done.

The bottom line is – tell me any other property training programme that has created over 69 millionaires!

My client base includes investment bankers, architects and quantity surveyors all fed up with making other people money. In addition, there are aeroplane pilots, doctors, accountants, nurses, teachers, postmen and taxi drivers. The only thing they all have in common is the desire to make a positive change to their future.

*"Buying real estate
is not only the best way,
the quickest way,
the safest way,
but the only way
to become wealthy."*

Marshall Field

Who wants to be a millionaire?

So who wants to be a millionaire? As a television show at its peak, it attracted 19 million viewers but how many millionaires did it actually create? In the fourteen years that the show ran in the UK, only five people ever won the top prize of £1m. But in television, the saying went that the only people it really turned into millionaires on a regular basis were its producers.

With a total of 69 so far, I can proudly boast that I have turned vastly more people into millionaires than the show ever did. However, five years ago I was once challenged to see if I could choose someone at random and turn them into a millionaire. In fact, I was bet a whole one pound that I couldn't. Of course, I couldn't resist!

Shortly after that, I was running one of my events in a hotel with 173 people in the audience and I thought I would give it a go. At the end of my training, I invited everyone to put their name into a hat. I drew out five names and invited each of them up on stage to interview them. From the five, I picked one – Sean Brett. I invited him to come onto my programme free of charge and become a millionaire. He started his property career with just £12,000 he had raised from friends and family. Now, five years and a few months later, he is now an equity/cash millionaire. Of course, it was all to avoid having to pay back that initial one pound bet!

Here is Sean's story in his own words.

Sean Brett

I suppose everyone's journey is different. Mine started 10,000 miles away in the sunny eastern province of KwaZulu Natal in South Africa. I was born in Durban and grew up on a sugar farm 100km north near a lovely place called Zinkwazi Beach where I spent most of my weekends paddling away in the surf.

I went to university in the late 1990s to do a BCommand then did a bit of travel, as you do. I've always had a passion for travel and exploring new cultures. I later studied IT and networking systems so when I moved back to the UK in 1999, I had no trouble in getting a post as an IT manager with a big telecoms company in London. In 2001, I hit the road again traveling overland from Europe to Australia, where I spent a year.

Back home, my father had taken an interest in property and property education and had bought a handful of properties; he believed it was a good investment vehicle. It was always in my mind to do the same as a tool for my retirement. I studied authors like Robert Kiyosaki 'Rich Dad, Poor Dad' and others. For me, personal development was really important.

In 2006, I found myself back in the UK to help set up a European sales channel for a South African technology company. In 2009, I bought my first property in the UK with a friend, which had given me a bit of seed capital but I really wasn't sure what to do next. I spent near enough the next 18 months and many a weekend or weekday evening at free property seminars without buying another property. Mostly out of fear of getting it wrong and tying up the seed capital.

I remember that I had invested (rather than given up) a Monday night to travel to the Berkshire property meet. Tony, one of Glenn's ambassadors, was there. It was a result of meeting and talking to him that I attended a competition that Glenn was holding in late 2010 where somebody would win free mentorship over three to five years, however long it took, from wherever they were starting out until they reached £1 million in equity. Boy, was I going to make sure I was there, and yes, I was fortunate enough to win and I joined Glenn's 12-month mentorship programme pro bono. It was exactly what I needed and I immersed myself in it. There were weekly webinars and a monthly get-together in Milton Keynes, plus a wealth of priceless information.

One of the initial challenges that Glenn set me was to research five high-yielding cities in the UK that I might want to work in, and then spend a day there getting to know the local market. Wherever you get your first property deal, that is where you settle. So off I went, and over the five to six days, I managed to see some 60 or 70 properties, around ten per day – believe me, I was working hard and determined to crack this thing. I wasn't coming back empty-handed!

I finished up in Bristol. At first, the offers I had put in were cringingly low as I had Glenn's voice in my ear saying, "If you're not embarrassed with the price you are offering, it is too high!" Fortunately, I had also remembered my training and said to one estate agent, "We can also help people who are being repossessed or are in arrears by paying off there arrears, then agree a sale in the near future." He said, "Hang on, I think I have someone who is in exactly that situation," and that's exactly what we did for them.

For me, that was a good learning point. Always aim to understand the seller's problem and match them up with a win-win solution.

Sometimes it might be about speed of sale and they may have equity to part with and can compromise on price, other times there may be no equity but they would like to move and leave the debt behind and will agree to your terms if you take care of the bigger issue and offer them their required price. Property education will give you a toolbox of strategies that you can implement to find the win-win in most situations.

So back to our first Bristol deal. The estate agent phoned the gentleman up and invited him into the office to see how I might be able to help him.

He had two properties that were in arrears by some £8,000 and was facing repossession in the following four weeks. One was a three-bedroom house that was cash flowing but not very well. The other was a much larger four-bedroom, three-reception, which was making money and that he wanted to hang on to. I asked Glenn for his advice.

At that time, I was living in London in rented accommodation. Glenn took this into account with his advice. We had to offer on both properties or neither and then make sure the seller gets what he needs. I agreed to pay off his £8,000 arrears in return for a five year lease on both properties and pay him what he was asking in today's money. He was delighted as he was just two steps away from being repossessed. He also knew that this meant within five years he would receive £30k from the one property and £15k from the other property. He was nearing retirement age and this was a huge burden off his shoulders. We signed the deal. I went to court with an N244 form and had the repossession stopped. It felt good. This would be the first of many times in court stopping repossessions.

I was now responsible for £1,500 in mortgages plus the rent of our London flat. We quickly handed in our notice and moved into the larger of the two properties, which we turned into an HMO.

It gave us space for an office and we were able to live and work there rent-free. My wife was still a nurse in London at that time, but she could see the big picture of what we were doing and was prepared to work shifts and commute, whilst staying in a bed and breakfast for a couple of days per week. It was less than ideal, but it enabled us to achieve our objective and I could focus on property full time.

In the end, I assigned the option to buy on the first property for £20,000 and the property sold netting the vendor £30k as promised. Everybody was happy. The other property I have recently purchased outright and refurbished it into a five-bed, all en-suite HMO and it is still part of my portfolio today.

Meanwhile, in Bristol, I was still putting into practice what I was learning through the Mastermind group. I was systematically learning the tricks of the trade of the property world and how to legally buy with no money down; how to do delayed completion and lease options etc. It was great to be surrounded with people who were doing these things every day and were happy to share their knowledge and experience. There is no doubt that it speeded up my business growth no end.

I kept on working on my marketing 'funnel' in the Bristol area and developed a relationship with a number of estate agents who were on the lookout for properties that matched our criteria. I also spend a lot of time looking for off-market opportunities. When you put yourself out there and market your services, the opportunities will arise. If you invest in your education, you will maximise your chances of converting each opportunity. I also put a lot of effort into streamlining our processes and systems. If you know that your office systems, accounting system, bookkeeping and property management are running smoothly, you can concentrate on those IGT (income generating tasks) of the business. Getting bogged down in penny tasks simply steals your time – and that is far too valuable to waste!

It took me five years to reach the £1 million target, and my new goal is to double that within two years. The focus now will be on development and new builds. I do not tell that to you to impress you but to impress upon you that you can reach your goals within reasonable time frames with the right mix of education and hard work. I know some people who have done it much faster and others that have made no progress at all. It's not a race, it's a journey.

To do that, I have had to have a mindset change and remove myself from the everyday noise. My systems make that possible. I now have a Virtual Assistant in the Philippines who works 20 hours a week for me doing research and admin. I also have a Personal Assistant who is my property manager. She does all my viewings, check-ins and check-outs, property maintenance and inspections. You can imagine what a load that is off my shoulders. This also allows us to travel knowing that everything will continue to work as it should without me. This is an added bonus and in part the reason for getting into property in the first place.

If you are starting out in property, my advice would be to get properly educated by people who are successfully doing what you want to do. There are enough of them.

Run away from people who are all theory and no track record! Go to your local property investor network events. Find a mentor that you like to work with. You don't know what you don't know.

I will always be grateful to Glenn for his personal interest in me and the ongoing advice he has given me at every stage.

*"Ambition is the
path to success.
Persistence is the
vehicle you arrive in."*

Bill Bradley

Mik Patel

My parents arrived in the UK as immigrants from India in the 1970s. I was born into a large family and all of them seemed to be into property in one way or another, some as their principle business and others more as a hobby. I would see family members buying and 'flipping' a property, or buying and holding, but all of it done in a very 'old-school' way without any clever strategies. It was all a part of my education growing up.

My father bought many commercial and residential properties over a 40-year period but not in an expansive way. In fact, what my father did in over 40 years I am now planning to do over one, thanks to Glenn. But let me start at the beginning.

I was always ambitious and competitive. My original dream was to go into medicine and I was fortunate enough to qualify to go to Cambridge University to study it. By now, I could have been a doctor but halfway into the course, I decided that it wasn't for me and left. At that time, I wasn't really sure what was for me, so I did a bit of travelling to try and find out.

When I returned, I managed to get a job with a tier 1 US investment bank, and for the next ten years I was on the trading and sales desk in the fixed income markets. I loved the job but it had its downsides. There were 5 a.m. starts, a lot of travel and late evenings doing client hospitality. It sounds glamorous but the reality is that it wasn't and it was not the healthiest of lifestyles!

After the credit crunch of 2009, banker remuneration was not the same and bonuses were also smaller. I became disillusioned and I *left with a view to finding a new direction in life or a new business that would help me to achieve my goals.*

By this time, I had already dabbled in property but just as a sideline. Old family habits die hard. I started to think that maybe I should look at it full time. If I were to do this, I knew that I would need to do it in a far more structured and strategic way than my family had done in the past, and look to build a business from the ground up. I started to do my research to find out who were to main movers and shakers in the market. It didn't take long to find out.

I was looking for a mentor to work with. Someone I could trust and respect; someone who had a track record of success; and someone who was an innovator in the industry. I had attended a number of different courses given by a number of property experts, but nothing had really gelled for me. Then I found myself at the London networking event where I heard Glenn speak for the first time. He was very down to earth with no glitzy showmanship but this more than made up for the quality and depth of what he was talking about. What struck me immediately was his clever strategies for both property and business. He thought like an investment banker would think, which is very rare.

Mentally, I had made the decision to work with him, but first I bought his DVD set to really tune into his way of thinking. I watched them all and I was convinced. I called the office and joined his next four-day programme. After the first day, I signed up for his mentorship programme with a view to upgrading to his partnership programme – which I did a week later!

I have never looked back! I believe that, once you have done your research and made a decision, you need to then take action and get on with it. Life is not a rehearsal!

I had clear goals about what I wanted to achieve. I needed to maintain a level of financial freedom that allowed me to travel a lot. In fact, one of the reasons that I left banking was that I only had 28 days' holiday a year and could only take a maximum of two weeks at a time. Not enough!

One of the other aspects of working with Glenn is his emphasis on personal development. He has a list of books that he considers essential reading if you are to cultivate a real success mindset. I was pleased to see that I had already read most of them before joining his programme. I felt very much on his wavelength.

What really opened my eyes though was when I worked with him on creating my business plan and started to apply his innovative way of thinking and his business strategies to my own business. All of a sudden, I realised that I had a far greater potential than I realised. From my banking days, I had accumulated a good nest egg, so now was the time for it to hatch!

During my time with Glenn, my business has matured and grown beyond recognition. I am now moving into developments and still learning all the time. All I can say is that, if you are considering working with Glenn, do not hesitate. The basis for everything he does it that it has to be win-win for it to work. I believe that is the key to his personal success. The fact that he has helped 69 ordinary people achieve extraordinary results and become millionaires in their own right speaks for itself.

"Persistence is to the character of man as carbon is to steel."

Napoleon Hill

Chapter Eleven

Choosing your right strategy

In tailoring, one size does not fit all. In property, it is the same. There is no point just copying a strategy that someone else is getting results from; it may not be right for you, your circumstances, the area you live in, or want to work in. So as you listen and learn from others, and take part in our seminars and events, think of the knowledge that you are getting in the same way as the sweets on the Poundshop's pick 'n' mix counter. Pick the flavours that suit you!

I have seen people getting excited about one strategy and trying it – for a month. They then hear about something else and try that instead. If you flit from one thing to another, you are never going to make money. Property is a long-term game and the decisions you take should be given long enough to work. Avoid being distracted by 'shiny pennies' and concentrate of the strategy you have chosen.

Be aware that, when choosing your strategy, each strategy doesn't necessarily work in every part of the country. There are local factors to take into account. By focusing your property portfolio in one geographical area, not only are they easier to manage and keep an eye on, but you are building up knowledge of what works in your area. Good local knowledge can give you a real edge along with building up relationships with agents and referrers which is essential.

Resist the temptation to rush into things and start buying properties without having clarity on:

- where you are going to operate;

- what strategy you are going to use;

- what marketing you will need to do;

- what demographics you will be marketing to; and

- what marketing materials you will use for your chosen demographics.

There is no substitute for having a well-thought-out plan, no matter how enthusiastic you may be to get started. One of the advantages of our courses is that you will be meeting and mixing with people at different stages of their property journey and who already have clarity on what works for them. By talking to them, you will also pick up some nuggets of gold to help you to arrive at your own conclusions.

You will also learn about the different property 'microclimates' around the country where some strategies work better than others – and some don't work at all! There is a heavy price to put for ignorance!

Chapter Twelve

Setting your business goals

Why is it that people groan at the mention of goals. It is that people think, "Oh I know this stuff," and mentally glaze over – or move on to the next chapter? Is it that they were forced to set goals in the past and didn't find it helpful? Or is it that they know that goal setting works, but they don't want to subject themselves to the discipline?

For many people, they are starting their property investment career part-time and are already busier than they can cope with. The thought of the work involved in setting time-sensitive goals that require time to achieve, and fitting that in around everything else, is a step too far. But before you start to search for a plausible excuse for not setting goals, and before you get a letter from a responsible adult to excuse you, think on this.

> ## *"If you don't know where you are going, you will probably end up somewhere else."*

You need to plan for what your success is going to look like so you know when you get there!

The big picture

Before you start anything, you need to know what the result is going to be. What will be the reward for all of your hard work? One way of doing this is to create your own vision board.

A vision board will give you a daily reminder of your 'Why' so it is important that you position it somewhere that you will see it regularly. It could be on your fridge or on a framed cork board on the wall of your office. It could even be on the inside of the door to the smallest room in the house. You choose!

Some people will cut out pictures from magazines of the things they want to own or places they want to visit. My early vision board would have certainly included pictures of the prestige cars that I now own. It may even have included the type of house which I now own. You see, vision boards work!

What is your motivation? What does it take to get you out of bed? What will you reward your success with when it arrives? You need to know what it is, you need to visualise it and you need to be reminded of it every day.

They say that you become what you think about the most. Certainly we do attract into our lives those things we are focused on. It is know as 'The Law of Attraction'. The best way to understand this is to watch the film *The Secret*.

The Secret is a bestselling self-help book first published in 2006 and written by Rhonda Byrne. It was based on the earlier film of the same name.

The Secret is all about the Law of Attraction and claims that positive thinking can create life-changing results such as increased happiness, health and wealth. The book has sold more than 19 million copies worldwide and has been translated into 46 languages. It has attracted a great deal of controversy and criticism for its claims, and has been parodied on several TV programmes. So what is the Law of Attraction?

Although the theory behind the Law of Attraction is very simple, putting it into practice on a conscious level takes work. Negative and limiting belief systems are buried deep inside us. Changing or ridding yourself of ideas and old habits that defeat you at every turn is possible. Are you up to the challenge? Start by learning how to break the habit of attracting negatives.

The creative process as portrayed in the extended version of the movie *The Secret* involves three steps to attracting all your desires.

- Ask – You must know what you want. I mean, really know what you want. The universe can't deliver without first knowing what it is that you want to have manifested into your life.

- Believe – You need to truly believe that what you are asking for will become yours. Doubts need to be pushed away. The idea that failure is a possibility will mess up the delivery.

- Receive – It is important that you become an active player in reaching your goals. When opportunity comes your way, you must not hesitate. Grab the opportunity when it appears.

Some people believe in this wholeheartedly, and other people think it's a load of mumbo jumbo. What I can say to you is that if you put it into action, things will start happening, strange things that may or may not have ever occurred to you before. So how does the Law of Attraction work? And why should you set yourself goals?

By setting the goals, it means that you actually know what you're striving for, and then by breaking it down, it's much easier to achieve your goals. When you have actually set your goals towards what it is that you are trying to achieve, things will start happening. This is why the vision board is so important to help you achieve your goals.

*"To be successful,
you have to be willing
to be successful.
You have to believe in
the law of attraction -
that you create your own life."*

Ted Danson

Making it work for you

So how can you tap into this powerful concept? You start with the end in mind. Let's imagine that you've got a Sat Nav. Unless you programme in the destination you want to go, you're not going to go anywhere because the Sat Nav won't work. Imagine me as your Sat Nav. You programme in where you want to be. I can look at where you are now, where you want to be and I can say, "Look, first do this, then do this, then do this, and move on. We can break it down into small bits and we can break it into weekly tasks."

You've got to know what your end goal is. The most important thing that drives successful people is having a huge reason 'Why'. If you've got a reason for doing things, then things happen. That's why you have the vision board. You put on there all the things you want for your future, and you will get what you ask for. Please don't put, 'I want to get out of debt', because if you put that, you'll get what you put. You'll get debt. Put things like, 'This is a copy of my bank statement in five years,' and have a quarter of a million or half a million pounds on the bank statement. That's the way to present it on your vision board.

Start with the end in mind. Create your own vision board. Once you've got your vision board, you set your goals and then we do a step-by-step plan of how to get there. This is called a business plan.

In fact, you need to have clarity not just on one goal, but on multiple goals. Yes, you will probably have one big goal on what you want to achieve in one or more years and what that means to you in terms of money, the number of properties you have or the lifestyle it has made possible. But in order to achieve that within the timescale you have identified, you will need to have shorter time milestones which will let you know that you are on track.

I am a great believer in linking short-term goals to activity. It is easy to measure what you do and the results it achieves. This knowledge give you the ability to see what is working and what isn't on a monthly basis and to make whatever in-flight course corrections you need to make in order to stay on track.

For example, if your strategy is to use leafleting in an area in order to find properties to buy, you need to find out what the conversion ratio of leaflets to enquiries is and the number of enquiries to sales.

"You cannot manage what you do not measure."

Initially, you may set a goal of delivering (or having delivered on your behalf) a few thousand leaflets in your target area. You need to record where and when. You need to record the result you achieved. Now you have some data to work with. Say that for every 1,000 leaflets, you received one phone call, and for every 20,000 leaflets, you made one high discount purchase. You now know what to expect next time. It also means that if you needed to buy two houses this month, you need to put out 40,000 leaflets. Of course, these figure are arbitrary, but you get the idea. If you set specific goals, and put the activity in to achieve them, you will get predictable results.

Every aspect of your business is capable of being measured. If you can then relate that activity to results, you are now able to plan for your growth.

Once you have set your big goal of where you want to be in, say, three years' time, you then work backwards from that to identify where you will need to be in two years, or one year, in order to be on track. You then break your one year goal down in to 12 monthly goals, and you then know what you need to do in the next four weeks to be certain of achieving your big goal in three years' time. It is not rocket science, but it is a discipline. In my view, if you are serious about becoming a millionaire, goal setting is an essential discipline you will need.

> ## *"You don't become a millionaire by accident. You become a millionaire by <u>planning</u> to become one."*

If you are serious about becoming a millionaire as a result of your property business, then you will need to treat it as a business and not as a hobby. It is the discipline of setting goals, doing the necessary activities to achieve them, and monitoring your results. This the difference that will make the difference with your results.

Once you have studied all of the strategies I teach on my courses, and what type of areas they work in, you will be able to decide on realistic goals – goals that you can achieve in your own time frame. You will then be able to write a business plan for yourself.

This plan will include:

- what your goals are;

- how you are going to get from where you are now to your goals;

- what time frame you will do it in;

- what strategy you will use; and

- what location you will work in.

By joining one of my courses, and by following my suggestions, within a short period of time you will get clarity on all of this and be able to plan to achieve your goals. Once you've decided on your strategy and your area, there's a series of other things that you need to do to follow through. When you follow through in the right order, you'll be able to do more, find more deals and make more money.

Some of the other important factors I cover includes identifying your buying criteria for each strategy. You may need to have a different buying criteria for each chosen strategy.

If you're working on two or three strategies, it might be that you've got several different buying criteria. I explain this in more detail on the courses.

It's important that you choose the correct buying criteria. This is because when a prospective property purchase appears, you'll be able to see immediately that it fits, and you can say, "Yes, I'll buy it," rather than spending three or four days trying to decide whether that one is for you, and running the risk of losing the opportunity to buy because another buyer has moved faster than you.

You will also need to understand the fundamentals of marketing. Marketing is vital; your choice of marketing technique will bring your deals in. Good marketing will allow you to do deal after deal, so we'll be looking at the different types of marketing methods that are available and how these will create successful deals for you.

We'll also look at how to negotiate with the vendors. It's key that you follow the negotiation methods I teach you. I have produced a step-by-step process for you to follow with the exact words and language that you can use. I know from past experience that kids are great negotiators. I also know at one point in time, you were a kid. So, therefore, it's definitely in you to be a great negotiator!

For example, my son will come to me and say, "Dad, can I borrow the car tonight?" I'll agree.

A little bit later, he'll come up and say, "Dad, can I borrow £30 or £40 to go out with tonight?" And I'll say, "Yeah, okay."

Then when he comes and says, "Can I have the car keys and that £40?" I give it to him, and he'll say, "Is it alright if I stay out until 3 a.m.?" Now, that's the negotiation! That's what I call the nibbling technique – bit by bit. At no point would he ever come and say, "Dad, can I borrow £30 or £40 and borrow the car and stay out until 3 a.m.?" It just wouldn't happen.

So when you follow the nibbling process we've developed, you will be able to negotiate deal after deal. With these finely honed negotiating skills, you can get discounts of 15%, 20%, 30%, even up to 50%, below the market value of that property.

You will also need to learn to do 'due diligence'. Before you buy something, it's very important that you understand the dynamics of what you're buying. What is the area really like? Is the price right? What are the timescales when you come to sell? These factors will vary depending on which strategy you have chosen to use.

The journey to becoming a first-class and successful property professional is a step-by-step process. Yes, there is a lot to learn, but on my courses and in my mentoring programme we make sure you get the support you need every step of the way.

Chapter Thirteen
Skills you will need to succeed

Communication

The ability to communicate well, in a timely and unambiguous manner, is vital to your success in all businesses, but in the world of property investment and development in particular. Property is a world where thing happen fast and opportunities present themselves fleetingly. The ability and the tools to react immediately are what makes the difference. Gone are the day when people checked their emails once a day, whether they needed to or not. Being always connected is now expected. Those that are have a huge advantage over those that are not.

Do a communications audit.

- How easy are you to be found and contacted?

- Are there alternative ways to contact you on your website?

- Are your emails synced with your smartphone?

- Do you present a professional front with your emails, both from your mobile devices as well as your office PC?

- Do you use a personal email or a business email address?

- Do you use a branded email signature?

- Does it have all the various ways you can be contacted?

- Do you have an intelligent messaging service you can switch to when you are busy?

- What impression do people have when they contact you? Is it the impression you want to create?

Remember, you only have one chance to make a first impression! Everything after that is trying to repair the damage!

Some organisations I have contacted seem to have a very efficient 'Sales Prevention Department' geared up to stop a potential customer from getting through. I am sure that they weren't set up with this in mind, but that is certainly the result. A phone continually set to answerphone and messages left unanswered puts out a powerful message – we are too busy for your business, please go elsewhere. And people do.

Whilst I am not advocating that you are personally available 24/7, you do need to make sure that you have a system in place so that an urgent opportunity doesn't get brushed away and left on a desk somewhere for you to find later. You need to be able to be contacted, even if you put a filter in place.

I use a professional answering service for when I am busy. They answer with my business name, are well briefed and have plenty of information at their fingertips. They also know who to contact in my organisation should the need arise.

Hidden messages

The way you communicate says a lot about you, your values and the culture of your organisation. In all organisations, this emanates from the top. The way you communicate to them is the way you communicate to everyone else. Never forget that the words you use are only a small part of the message you are communicating.

Visual and Non-Visual communication.

We are all putting out messages all of the time, even if we are saying nothing. People will look at the way we dress, our posture, gestures, the way we position ourselves, and walk. They will read messages into everything. It is impossible to be one thing, and communicate something completely difference. You need to be congruent in everything.

Amazingly the actual words when we are talking represent as little as 7% of the message that people receive. Around 38% of our communication is delivered by the tone and pitch of our voice, and the remaining 55% by our body language. The good news is that it is the same for everyone else!

A great skill to learn is the ability to 'read' people and to understand what they are really saying. Whether you are talking to banks and mortgage professional, house sellers, potential tenants or indeed anyone else, developing the skill of interpreting the combination of all their simultaneous messages will help you make the right decision and work with the right people.

In my recommended reading list, you will find Desmond Morris' intriguing book *The Naked Ape*. Your exploration into human communication could not start in a better place

The Greatest Fear

One of the other forms of communication that you will need to become fluent and confident in is public speaking. There will be times when you need to make a presentation or talk to a group of people. The outcome might be very important to you, and you will only have one chance to pull it off.

Here are some thoughts to consider.

- Be well prepared. You need to know what you need to say in a logical sequence: opening, main points, summary. Put another way, tell them what you are going to tell them, then tell them, and lastly tell them what you told them!

- Practice and rehearse a speech frequently prior to delivering it. Ask friends to be your audience, or practice in front of a mirror. Be sure to use a timer to help you pace your speech. Never over run your time!
- Become familiar with the stage or the setting where

the speech will take place. Get a sense of the size of the stage, where any steps or obstacles might be, and where to enter and exit. Will there be a sound system? Get there early enough to find out!

- Choose comfortable clothes to wear, but always maintain a professional appearance.

- Visual aids should fit the speech, whether they are funny, serious or technical. The main goal of visual aids is to help the audience understand what is being said, and reinforce the points of a speech in unique and interesting ways. Never stand there and read the words from a PowerPoint presentation.

- Ideally you would want to get eye contact with each section of the audience during your presentation.

- After you have summarised what you have just said, always finish by repeating your name and a thank to them for listening.

"If you're not comfortable with public speaking – and nobody starts out comfortable; you have to learn how to be comfortable – practice.
I cannot overstate the importance of practicing."

Hillary Clinton

Are you a social animal?

Incredibly it is less than a decade since smartphones started to take over our lives. The growth in connectivity, going from 2G to 4G and now 5G, has meant that we can now easily get video on the move and also connect with all of the social media platforms.

If you are not currently using social media, and think it is a waste of time, then think again. Social media is all about creating a personal network of people who share the same interests. Indeed many people do just use it to exchange trivia but equally many people do use some social media platforms to build serious businesses.

If you want to be known as the go-to person for property in your area, and to attract potential tenants or sellers, the best place for that is to be found where they hang out. It might not be your place of choice for communicating, but if it is for the people you want to meet, then your personal preferences are irrelevant!

Decide what you want to be known as and what solution you deliver, then start to grow your presence. You'll be surprised how quickly you can build a group of people who want to know more or who are looking for something you can provide.

If this is a new world to you, you'll probably need a seven-year-old to set it up for you, but it is worth it. Firstly, it is a free way to reach literally millions of people. Secondly, if you set yourself up properly, they will find you rather than you go in search of them.

Are you invisible?

These days you are as good as invisible if you don't come up on the first page of Google. It is a good exercise to do a search for yourself and see what is there. Whilst you are at it, do make a point of checking Google images as well! If there are some unfortunate pictures of you taken on a stag night, you might want to be aware of them now and do something about it, before an important client finds them first!

If you are going to position yourself as an expert, you need to be found online in that capacity with an effective website. You may well have other websites for your businesses, but if you want people to search for you, you'll need to make it as easy as possible for them to find you.

These days when you speak to somebody for the first time on the phone, they are quite likely to be Googling you and looking for your website during the conversation to get confirmation of what you are saying. If they don't find what they are looking for, it can harm your credibility.

You need to have clarity on what you want to be found for, what you deliver, and the problems you solve. You don't require anything complicated or expensive but your website must reflect your brand values, be easy to navigate, and make it easy for people to do business with you.

Your website is your shop window and your business card. It is essential to your success.

The need for a mentor

Vivek Wadhwa is an American technology entrepreneur and academic, and the author of the 2014 book *Innovating Women: The Changing Face of Technology*. He once said "What you want in a mentor is someone who truly cares for you and who will look after your interests and not just their own. When you do come across the right person to mentor you, start by showing them that the time they spend with you is worthwhile."

You would be hard pressed to find anyone who has made it to the big time in any profession who didn't have one or more mentors to help them on their way. I know that I did.

Having a mentor is not a sign of weakness. It is not an admission that we are in some way inadequate. On the contrary, it is the acknowledgement that we are all on a journey of continuous learning and growth. No matter what stage we are at professionally, there will always be people who know more and have had a wider range of experiences. To find someone who you respect and who is prepared to share that knowledge and experience to help you on your way, is invaluable.

I take our mentorship programme very seriously. I know what it was like when I started my property business. I made all the mistakes and sometimes I was lucky. I didn't know what I didn't know! But I do know that, had I had the right mentor, then it would have made all the difference. I have a responsibility to share what I now know and to help all of my mentees achieve the all the success they are capable of.

Masterminding

Being a property investor and developer can be a lonely place Everything rests on you and your decisions. Taking a wrong decision can be costly. On top of that, you will have developed your own unique strategy based of your personal objectives, in the area you have chosen to work. Nobody else has a business exactly like yours.

The support, knowledge and encouragement of other investors in your peer group can also play a vital part in your success. This is why I have built a Masterminding elements into our courses and programmes. I have found that there is a wonderful dynamic of sharing and support that comes from when people work and grow together on my courses. Far from being in competition with each other, people get inspired by the success of others and are only too willing to share what they did and what they learned.

We continue this after the courses with our webinars and group calls and have created mastermind groups as a result. I believe that this has played a big part in creating so many property millionaires out of our courses. We now have a very supportive community of talented and successful people, all intent on being the best they can be, and willing to support and encourage others on their journey.

*"If you're trying to achieve,
there will be roadblocks.
I've had them;
everybody has had them.
But obstacles don't have to stop you.
If you run into a wall,
don't turn around and give up.
Figure out how to climb it,
go through it, or work around it."*

Michael Jordan

Chapter Fourteen
Have you got what it takes?

It is a fact of life that not everyone who attends my courses becomes a millionaire. It is the same in every walk of life. Not everyone qualifies to be a doctor, or an engineer for that matter. It is not that they couldn't, but there was something standing in their way. In many cases, they put it there themselves. What I can guarantee is that, by attending one of my courses, we will find out if there is anything standing in your way, and if so, you will receive help to remove it.

Of the 69 people (so far) that have become millionaires as a result of attending my course, and then deciding to take action, I have noticed that they come from all walks of life. Some of them had money to start with, others didn't. In fact, some of them were not even creditworthy. Each of them has unique circumstances, all of them had different goals, and all of them were determined to do what it took to succeed.

What I've seen is that you do not have to have any particular qualifications – but you do have to have particular values. Where you came from doesn't matter, only a strong desire to change where you are heading – and have a deep desire to take action to make that possible. Let me introduce you to some of my mentees who I have had the pleasure to work with. See if what you will learn from their stories can give you an insight into whether you are suited to do the same.

Nick Pedrithes' story

I know everyone comes into property from different directions and with different experiences. In most cases, including mine, my early career gave me little grounding in what I was subsequently going to do, but it did teach me a number of skills and qualities that have been invaluable. I grew up working in my father's restaurant – and I mean working. The fact that I was his son didn't mean I had an easy ride, quite the opposite! It was a huge Greek restaurant in Camden Town. The hours were incredibly long as our busiest time was between midnight and six in the morning. Amazingly, on a Saturday night we would serve over a thousand meals. I know that because, at the age of 12 I was given the responsibility of dish washing. I quickly found out what a thousand dinner plates looked like, and a thousand side plates, and a thousand dessert plates! Need I go on? I only wished that more of the customers would adopt the Greek tradition of smashing their plates as a sign that they enjoyed the meal. At least they wouldn't need to be washed.

In fact, my father put me into each area of the business, both front and back of house, to learn the trade. I got used to handling money in large amounts so it doesn't scare me today with the big deals we now do. I went through my education and university having to work four times harder than the others in order to get over my dyslexia. I had to take my GCSEs more than once because of it, but I persevered. I eventually got a degree in IT, something that really suited me, but every weekend when my fellow students were going out and getting drunk, I would be back in the restaurant working from dusk to dawn. I was now managing people three times my age in what was a tough and a somewhat robust working environment. Put it this way, you could swear by our food – certainly the chef had!

No better place to learn people skills and the art of good communication. The other good thing was that, because I had so little time to spend it, I was saving money and building up a nice little nest egg.

But I knew that the restaurant business was potentially a prison. I could easily have stayed there to this day with the long hours, but my degree in IT was my passport out. As it was to transpire, my knowledge of computing and systems was to made a dramatic difference to my present property business. More of that in a moment.

In my first IT job, I felt a bit of a fraud, probably because I had the qualifications but not the real world experience. I kept on working harder than everybody else, as I had always had to do in the past. I soon got really good in my field but that lurking sensation that this was just a fluke persisted and made me look around to find a second source of income, just in case the job didn't last. This fear that I wasn't really good enough pushed me to find something that would make me money whilst I was sleeping – not that I had much time for that!

I initially looked at stocks and shares but it was a world that I had no real experience in and it needed more time to put into it in order to succeed than I could really spare. That was when I started to look at the world of property.

By this point, I was married. Helpfully, one of the great traditions of a Greek wedding was that the guests pin money on the couple. This was a big help in getting my first mortgage, and of starting my property journey. By now, I was an IT contractor, a bit like a glorified temp, but very profitable! In fact, it only took me a few hours work at the beginning of each month to earn enough to clear my overheads and mortgage. The rest I used to build a cash reservoir to invest in property.

My first property was close to where I lived in Borehamwood, on the High Street above a shop. I put £20k down and it produced a yield of 7.2%. Spurred on by this, I repeated the process and got my second property. This time I put a council tenant in and started to build a good relationship with the council. As a result, I became a preferred supplier to them and they lined up 20 tenants for me right away.

Within a couple of years, I had bought five or six flats but I was beginning to realise that this was not sustainable as I couldn't buy the volume. By this time, I was in my early thirties, paying off my mortgage slowly, with a handful of properties, and still earning a substantial income from IT, but I realised that I had not yet hit critical mass and I needed to find out why.

I discovered that there was another world out there of property networking events. Why hadn't I found it before? I went along and this is where I met Glenn. My quest for knowledge was over! I started to find out all those things that, not only I didn't know, but I had never thought about before. What I was learning was going to make all the difference in catapulting my business forward.

I started to talk to Glenn regularly and all I would hear is him saying "I've just bought another one," again and again. How was he doing it? His average month was six new properties. I decided to take a big decision. As I had enough funds to allow me not to work for a couple of years, I cancelled my highly profitable IT contract and went to work for nothing at Glenn's office to grow my knowledge of the property business. It was the best thing I could have done.

So with renewed confidence, I started to market for properties, go out and view between ten to 15 in a month, but for some reason I couldn't close a deal. I discussed this with Glenn to get his advice. He agreed that, on paper, I was doing everything right, but as something obviously wasn't working, he agreed to come out with me to see the next property and to watch him at work. It was a masterclass, and I could see immediately where I had gone wrong.

My focus in the past had been on my objectives, what I wanted and the figures I needed to make it work. I quickly learnt that what I wanted was irrelevant. Nobody cared what I wanted, all they cared about was what they wanted – and that is what Glenn focused on. This was a real epiphany for me and it transformed my business.

As I watched for the first 20 minutes, Glenn just got to know them. He didn't talk about the property once. He then started to find out what they wanted by asking questions like, "So, at the end of this, what do you want the deal to look like? Do you want a cheap rent? Do you want cashback? Do you want to pay by credit card? Tell us what you want and I'll try and make it so that everyone is happy." With Glenn, it was win-win each time.

From that moment on, my success rate in closing took off. In the following six weeks, I closed some £700k of deals. I was now ready to move on and grow my business.

My next big lesson was in the way I managed my business. By now, we were growing fast and I was, in effect, a professional landlord. I had one member of staff and all the predictable problems associated with tenants and managing properties. I was busy doing refurbs and trying to keep all of the properties filled and income generating, only it wasn't quite working.

I stepped back and did some sums. I realised that I was haemorrhaging £15k per month. In fact, in a year I had accumulated losses of nearly £40k through lost rent and arrears. I had to act and quickly. Once again, Glenn's experienced eye helped me to identify where the problems were.

What helped me was my knowledge of IT and processes. I needed a system which would quickly pick up any variations from the norm so that a problem could be spotted quickly and resolved. I needed to know the numbers for each property and the 'what if' scenarios if something went wrong. I needed to systemise my back office, create spreadsheets and put myself firmly in the driving seat.

I also needed to have clear ground rules for my tenants so that they knew exactly where they stood if they didn't pay their rent. We needed an automated process which would be triggered as soon as a tenant was two weeks in arrears. I cannot afford to get emotionally involved. So, being fair to them, we instigated a system of text reminders which started two days after the rent was due. If they have a pattern of late payments, I text them four days before it is due. They always know where they stand and what will logically happen if they default.

I also introduced Key Performance Indicators into every aspect of the business so that we could quickly see trends and identify anything that was deviating from the norm. For me, this was the difference between working in my business to working on my business. A big lesson.

With my staff, I introduced quarterly audits. They have checklists to tick that they have completed each task, which they then sign to confirm. Today, because of the time I put into systems, my business *almost manages itself. I have as good team in place, with my wife running the back office and I work with a letting agent to manage the properties that are too far away from me. I have empowered my staff to take decisions based on our operations model, and we now have a very efficient machine. The regular monitoring of all the variables in each property have enabled us to identify profit leaks quickly and where utility bills are higher than average. This has also helped us to buy better and to negotiate bulk rates for gas, water and electricity.*

We have built up a network of people that I know, like and respect, and who share my values, who work with me on particular projects, and share their specialist expertise.

However, the biggest thing that I have learnt is to adopt a corporate mindset. Had I done this from the beginning, my business would look very different today. I now realise that it is not just about buying, but of managing each asset. It is about having controls in place because you cannot keep everything in your head. You need systems that know when a rent is due is and know whether it has arrived or not.

Systems that know when a refurb is due, when an inspection needs to be made. Unless you plan to do things, you are planning not to do things. Having robust systems in place makes sure that nothing falls through the gaps.

Finally, my advice would be to listen to Glenn. He often says, "You don't know what you don't know," and in property that is so true. There is no one way that is right, no template that you can follow and expect to succeed. It is not about simply having information, it is about learning from applied knowledge and you only get that from experience – either yours or someone else's.

In the world of property, everything is a variable – starting with you, your qualities, experience, skills, vision, attitude and drive. That is the reason that, when two people are presented with the same opportunity and set of circumstances, one succeeds and the other doesn't.

Your property business will be unique and will reflect the person you are, the strategy you are following and where you are working. It will also reflect the quality of the advice you are getting and the mentor you are working with. Anyone can become a one property accidental landlord, but if you are serious about making this a long-term successful business, you need the support and guidance of someone like Glenn who will stop you from making all the mistakes that are there, waiting for the unwary.

"You can get everything in life you want if you will just help enough other people get what they want"

Zig Ziglar

Phil Turtle's Story

My interest in property started when I was 19 and a student. Myself and two other students were at a polytechnic in Coventry. We had just completed our first year in the halls of residence and now needed to find somewhere to live. As luck would have it, three girls that we knew, and who shared a house together, needed to get house-sitters for the summer as they were going home. We jumped at it. Of course, we had to pay them rent, which was fair enough.

At some point during that summer, it dawned on me that, when they returned and we needed somewhere to move to, why not buy a house between us instead of paying rent and having nothing to show for it. The three of us agreed that it made sense and we set out to find one. With a bit of help from the bank of Mum and Dad, we managed to find enough to put a deposit down on a two-up, two-down, for the grand sum of £7,800. Those were the days!

All of us were practical as we were studying engineering or electrical engineering, so we all mucked in to install central heating, rewire and even to do a little structural work taking down a wall and removing a chimney. This was to be my 'blooding' in property.

I lived there for a few years, then a big 300-year-old cottage next door became available. It was a bit run-down but that didn't phase me having done so much to my existing house, so I bought it. As you do! I moved in and lived in the only habitable room as I proceeded to dig out earthen floors, install a damp course, putting down concrete slabs, underfilling, rewiring and replumbing and everything else.

I bought my original house for £7,800 and sold it to my other two partners for £8,500. By the time I had finished bringing it up to scratch, I sold it for £16,000. The cottage cost me £24,000, and four years later I sold it for £95,000. I now knew that this stuff worked!

Originally I met Glenn not at a property event, but at an NLP training event. We also bumped into each other at a number of personal development events. By then I had decided that I wanted to learn more about property and had already attended a number of the high-profile – and high-priced – property seminars that were all the rage at the time. What struck me with these events was that they were making all their money from doing training, not from building a property portfolio. For me, that didn't feel right. Knowing the theory is one thing, having experience at the sharp end of taking risks is completely another. With Glenn, he was doing just that, building a property portfolio first and foremost, and secondly doing some training and mentoring. For me, this has far more credibility.

Having kissed a few frogs along the way, I reconnected with Glenn to ask his advice about getting started in property, and he invited me onto his four-day course. I immediately knew I was in the right place. Unlike the glitzy property courses I had tried previously, this one had immediate credibility because of what Glenn was doing himself. There were no flash PowerPoint presentations and reams of statistics, just plain common sense based on an intimate knowledge of the marketplace and the experience of what works and what doesn't.

Having done property before on a hobby basis, I had complete confidence in my own abilities. I also had the range of skills require to upgrade a property myself. What I needed now was an understanding of strategy and the ability to assess a property and know if it was going to work as a profitable investment.

Fortunately, Glenn is very hands-on with his support, and over the next few months, he taught me what to look for in a property and how to weigh it up from a business perspective. He taught me that the bottom line is the bottom line. The only thing that matters is the numbers. Unless you have done your financial assessment and it works, there is no point in looking at anything else to do with it.

It is only too easy, if you are hungry to build a portfolio, to look at a property and just see pound signs, to ignore those inconvenient facts that stand in the way. Most people will look at a property from the perspective that they are going to live there. That is a completely different filter from looking at it as a business proposition.

For me, it took me six months before I found a property that met all the criteria. I had looked at many others leading up to it, but Glenn was able to point out something that I had overlooked which made them not viable. It is always down to the numbers. When you are talking about hundreds of thousands of pounds for a property, you only need one to fall out of bed to create a major problem. You have to get it right first time.

An example of this was a property I came across in Hastings. It was a big four-storey Victorian house, split in to flats. An agent I knew showed it to me with an asking price of £250,000. Using Glenn's magic formula, I worked out that the most I could afford to pay was £200,000, which I offered and got laughed at. It happens a lot! Eventually, they did get the asking price so I thought no more about it. A couple of months later, the agent called me to say that the sale had fallen out of bed, and that they might take £240,000. I said I was still interested, but only at £200,000. I had done all of the sums and I knew that if I paid any more, I would not make a profit.

One of the things that Glenn teaches is that, if you are not embarrassed by the offer you make, it is not low enough! I was not surprised when the offer was rejected. In fact, this happened another two times with other developers making offers, only for them to later pull out. Eventually, the agent came back to me to find out if my offer of £200,000 was still on the table. It was, so a year later I eventually purchased it.

I had estimated that the refurbishment would cost around £90,000 but as luck would have it, we discovered some well-hidden challenges. These included hot and cold rising damp, an infestation of beetles, and brick walls sitting on top of wooded beams, not steel joists. In fact, it became a real house of horrors! By now I had spent £210,000 instead of the £90,000 I had estimated. The profit had fallen from a potential £100,000 to £30,000 and even that was in doubt. I turned back to Glenn for advice It was sheer genius!

He suggested that the only way to rescue the situation was to make the flats more valuable. As it stood, the flats all had Victorian bay windows which afforded the odd glance at the sea, providing you stood in the right place. Glenn's imaginative solution was to create a glass tower at the front of the building to give large enclosed balconies for each flat giving panoramic views of the sea. He also suggested going up another floor to add another flat. This work has added more cost and time to the project, but now the profit is back up to £90,000, thanks to his good advice.

At this time, I was living in Brighton which has very high property prices and it's very difficult to make money as a result. Glenn's advice was to move to Hastings which had much more potential, lower prices and a lot of properties crying out to be refurbished. Again, I took his advice and have never looked back.

For me, the big advantage of working with Glenn is not just his personal experience and expertise, but also the fact that you are part of a mastermind group. Every week, you meet up with fellow investors and developers who are also working with Glenn, and discuss properties, strategies and solve problems together. Whilst on paper we all appear to be in competition with each other, the reality is that we are far more likely to cooperate on a project and work together, sharing our knowledge and skills. As a group, we regularly visit a property with Glenn and we all estimate what it would cost to refurbish it. It is a great exercise in observation. Missing one tiny clue can be very costly further down the line.

What I have learnt is that, to be successful in property, you do need to have good people skills. In fact, it is more about people than anything else. You need to be able to have good relations with estate agents and have them on your side, looking out for properties that meet your criteria. You will need to know civil servants in planning and building control, and understand how they work and arrive at their decisions. You will need to build relationships with builders, and a whole range of specialists. You will also need to be able to talk to potential house sellers, some of whom might be going though a difficult time, and to make them feel comfortable about doing business with you. It was no coincidence that I first met Glenn at a NLP course!

You will obviously need an aptitude for numbers, after all it is the numbers that control everything. More than anything, you will need to have a passion for what you are doing. Property is not a get-rich-quick scheme, it is more get-very-rich-slow, but if you do it right, it has been shown to be the best way to generate a return, no matter what the market or the economy is doing. But the biggest thing is to have the right mentor.

Looking back, I remember finding a property in Rye, down on the south coast. It had been recommended to me by a local agent. I had visited it, done all my due diligence, worked out the figures, and everything stacked up. I showed it to Glenn, expecting him to endorse it, but instead, to my surprise, he said that it wouldn't work. I didn't understand. He pointed out that, at the time, there was a stamp duty threshold of £250,000. Properties that were actually worth more than that were not selling for their value but were being marked down to below the stamp duty threshold. A hidden trap waiting for the unwary.

Making the jump from being an accidental landlord, a hobby developer or a first-time investor is a big one. With the numbers being so high, and there being so many variables, my advice is – don't try and do it on your own. Working with Glenn as my mentor, I have avoided a number of potential disasters which had the potential of wiping me out had they gone wrong. Never forget, 'you don't know what you don't know'.

"The difference between a successful person and others is not a lack of strength, not a lack of knowledge, but rather a lack of will."

Vince Lombardi

Neil Thomas's Story

Without a shadow of a doubt, it was one nugget of gold that I learnt from Glenn that unlocked my property business. When I met him, I had already been within the industry for some ten years, but as a self-employed mortgage broker. Obviously, as a professional, I knew more about how the property market worked than cost, but from a completely different angle. As they say, it is what you learn once you know it all that make the difference. That was the case with me.

I was wearing my mortgage broker hat when I attended a property networking meeting in Birmingham. To be honest, I was out looking for business. At that time, I had five buy-to-let properties of my own which I had bought with 50% deposits, as you did in those days. What was in the back of my mind was to increase my property portfolio but I wasn't sure how I was going to do that because I couldn't afford any more deposits. I met Glenn at the event and we exchanged business cards. As a result, he added me to his mailing list and from then on, I received regular invitations to his events, which I ignored!

However, one of his invitations was to a seminar about buying properties at below market value at a hotel in Milton Keynes, which interested me, so I went along.

Despite everything I knew and had been trained on, there were still some gaps in my knowledge. I could see what some people were doing – and they made it seem easy but I couldn't quite put all the pieces together. Glenn fixed that in an instant!

The secret to buying below market value properties, he taught, was to use the discount as the deposit. The penny dropped and I now knew how it was done. As a result of that one tiny thing, my business took off.

Following that, we managed to purchase 29 properties in around 18 months, so a dramatic change. We ended up with a portfolio at that time of over three quarters of a million. The good thing is that, despite the fact that the market has gone though some big swings in the interim, and prices did fall back, I still have all of those properties today.

Of course, back in 2006 to 2007, the strategy was all about empire building. As long as a property generated a profit of around £150 a month, we were happy because we believed the value of a property would double every ten years. Those were the days! The reality turned out to be very different.

So, the strategy has to be, if you can't rely on the market to increase the value of your property, you have to add the value yourself by making improvements.

Property has always been a long-term business and I have seen huge fluctuations over the years, but if you build your portfolio correctly, you can weather the storms by changing your strategies to suit the economic conditions at the time.

With the knowledge I had built up, I was now doing refurbs to generate lumps of cash from projects, and joint venturing to do conversions into HMOs. I am now full-time in my property business which enables me to keep my finger on the pulse.

I am very fortunate that many of the tenants I put in at the beginning are still with me, some of them for almost ten years. My focus for them is to always keep the property at its best. I take maintenance very seriously and have a schedule of preventative maintenance and upgrades.

I have always got a whiteboard full of maintenance jobs and my tenants know that I care about them and the property. I am sure this is one of the reasons I have such loyal tenants. Skimping on maintenance, I believe, is very short-sighted. I see many small landlords trying to cut corners and do the absolute minimum. In my view, it will cost them far more in the long-term, and the value of their properties will suffer.

As it is no longer the case that you can bank of the value of a property doubling in ten years, you have to increase value in other ways. Good maintenance is one – and it always attracts a better quality of tenant.

**"To be successful in property,
you must always and consistently
put your clients' best interests first.
When you do, your personal needs will be
realized beyond your greatest expectations."**

Anthony Hitt

Marc Bringmann

I wasn't a property novice when I met Glenn. I'd done some serious training with another company: a year of study in 6 modules. I had plenty of theoretical knowledge, but I hadn't yet taken the plunge – and when I listened to Glenn speaking, I realised why. Theoretical knowledge can only take you so far. I needed something more, and Glenn provided it.

Looking back, I was a bit too comfortable for my own good – earning decent money selling tech research. I wasn't happy or satisfied in the job and I knew I wanted more out of life... but it seemed risky to rock the boat.

Glenn spoke at a property developers' meeting and I liked his approach – although he clearly knew his stuff, he was a bit of a maverick, a creative thinker. I'm a car enthusiast, and I also noticed that when he put his car keys down on the table, there was a Rolls Royce key, a Bentley key, an Aston Martin key... so this was a man who walks the walk, as well as talking the talk.

A little while later I was talking to a very successful property developer and asked him how he'd started out. He'd been mentored by Glenn, he said, at monthly meetings in London. I started to think... and then life gave me a real kick in the seat of my pants. I was made redundant. It wasn't a happy experience and I ended up having to see a solicitor to resolve matters. But there were no excuses now for not making changes in my life that I knew were overdue.

I lost my job in May. In June I did Glenn's 4 day property course. For me it was a game-changer. I said to my partner: "'Right – we're going to go into property!" From the start, this was a totally different experience to the study that I'd previously done. It's very hands-on and 'real world'

– it's only when you apply what you know to practical situations that you truly start to learn. Glenn has real inner conviction, he knows his stuff, and he's given me the knowledge and the confidence to think and analyse.

On Day three of the course, Glenn encourages each person to send out a marketing email, right then and there. In my opinion, taking that action is what marks out who's really serious. So I did. Straightaway my phone starting ringing. And by 'straightaway', I mean exactly that – my phone rang in the classroom with Glenn.

I asked if I could step outside – and Glenn said no! He saw a great learning opportunity for the whole group. So I took the call right there and had the conversation live. And suddenly, I was in property.

I needed to replace my income, of course, and to do that, I needed to think strategically. That's exactly what Glenn taught me to do. I identified areas which might work for me and started looking for properties. I decided on Glasgow because I got a great response to my email campaign in the area, and my daughter was at the university so being based there would give me more chance to see her – a win/win for me and my family.

I started prospecting and brought about ten possible deals to Glenn. Glenn threw them out, which began to get frustrating. But I listened to his reasons, and learned from that. Finally I brought him a plan to buy a bungalow and split it into two semis. I'd considered paying 300k. Glenn said the deal would work at 250k.

I was nervous, and to be perfectly honest, that feeling never quite goes away. That's what it means to be in business for yourself – the highs are higher, and sometimes the lows can be lower. Independence isn't for everyone... but I found out that it's certainly for me.

I had no structure around me at all in the beginning, so I set up an SPV – that's a Specific Purpose Vehicle, a limited company which exists to work on one just one project. I put my power team in place, negotiated, settled on a purchase price of 262k and started the work.

Then two things happened. The first was that I underestimated the cost of the project. The second was that I underestimated the price at which I could sell! So I ended up making 99.5k profit after tax. Not quite the nice round 100... but it showed me what was possible, and I was hooked.

I can't say enough good things about Glenn and the support I received from him. For me, the biggest difference between him and plenty of other trainers out there is that when you work with Glenn, you get Glenn. He's on the phone to you himself, he's there at the meetings. He enjoys working with people and sharing his expertise and knowledge. He cares and he wants you to succeed. I think he feels a duty, having been successful himself, to send the elevator back down.

At the start, as I've said, he turned down quite a few of my ideas. He doesn't do that now – I take fewer proposals to him, and they're usually prospects that will work. Thanks to what I've learned on his mentoring programme, I make the right picks. That's why I wholeheartedly recommend Glenn as a trainer and mentor.

I'd give three pieces of advice if you're thinking of going into property. First – prepare for the unexpected. Having a mentor behind you, and lots of support to draw on, is vital and helps you to stay in control when things don't go quite as planned. When I was trying to connect a property just outside Glasgow to the water mains, I was faced with exactly this situation. Scottish Water will connect the pipe for you, but you have to locate it and do the digging. They gave us a map and told us the pipe was 3 feet down underneath a grass verge. We dug to 3 feet. Then we dug to 4 feet. No pipe. We asked Scottish Water again. Next they told us we might have to dig up the road. We did that. Still nothing. Then they said it might be under land owned by the property next door.

Three weeks later, we'd dug 10 feet down all the way from the house to the roadside. Scottish Water even sent along a water diviner – but he couldn't find the pipe either! Eventually we got permission to connect to a pipe from another property, which is unusual. At least we managed to get a refund for the cost of the extra work.

My second piece of advice is – go for it! It's a real case of 'feel the fear and do it anyway'. Life's too short to procrastinate. A sense of real fulfilment and achievement is out there – but it's going to be just beyond your comfort zone. And my third piece of advice is – reward yourself for changing your life. It could be a car, a watch, a holiday – but do something to make your success tangible. For me it was a car, of course... I bought the Aston Martin I'd dreamed of owning since I was 10. Even now I have to pinch myself when I see it on my drive.

I'm excited about my future and the journey that I'm on. My only regret is not taking Glenn's course 10 or 20 years ago. Nowadays I work very hard, but I choose when I want to do so. The financial rewards and the flexible lifestyle are beyond anything you can achieve in a job.

Says Glenn:

Mark repeated the first project with a very similar title split bungalow project and made £107,000 in his second year. Both years he only worked 4 days per fortnight! Mark has just purchased a large property for conversion into seven flats with a projected profit of £300,000.
Later in the year the has booked to fly to Perth Australia on the new Quantas Dreamliner and is not expected to return to the UK for three of four years.

Ian Lawson

I wasn't a property beginner when I met Glenn. I'd built up a portfolio worth around £8 million prior to the 2007 crash. I sold £3 million of it and basically retired to the Caribbean, which was wonderful.

So my partner and I travelled the world for four years. We enjoyed our lifestyle very much. Our business was still running with local staff and we could work from our laptops when we needed to. It sounds idyllic and in many ways it was, but a situation like that teaches you about yourself. By around 2011, I noticed that I was missing the more dynamics aspects of life. I enjoy work – the cut and thrust and challenge, something to feel passionate and energised around. One can only travel for so long.

So I decided to get back into the property game. I did a survey of all the property players and trainers in the UK. Because I had background knowledge, I was able to look at what was going on in some depth, and what I noticed was that quite a few operators are more show than substance – Wizard of Oz-type figures, where it looks impressive but there's no much going on behind the curtain. There are also plenty who are just running training businesses, and that's where they get their money from. I was looking for someone who was walking the walk, rather than just talking the talk.

But I also wanted somebody with absolute integrity who operates in a very authentic way. And I could immediately see, when I met Glenn at the Berkshire property meeting January 2011, that here I'd found what I was looking for.

First of all I was struck by his creativity and imagination. I'd honestly call it a genius that he has. Then there was an appeal on a different level. I'm an ethical person and my values are very important to me. I teach meditation and believe that it's very important to be aware of the wider dimensions of our actions. I'm not a religious person, but I am dedicated to making the world better and I was absolutely clear that I needed to work with someone who wasn't for sale. That's Glenn – I could see that immediately upon meeting him. I resolved there and then that we were going to be good friends.

I'd certainly had success before meeting him, but I was also aware at that time that you don't know what you don't know. This is something Glenn points out – but I already understood it. I could see that Glenn's business was larger than mine. I wanted to know what he knew, I wanted to be in a mastermind environment where he and I could bounce ideas off each other and where I could benefit from the energy and buzz that he creates. That was the downside of my four years' retirement – you can get quite comfortable. A bit too comfortable. Glenn certainly pulled me right out of that! Some of his strategies are genius, as I said before. He's cutting edge – he thinks ahead of his time. I welcomed that chance to be immersed in a dynamic environment. Basically – it was a kick up the arse!

Working with Glenn also gets you really clear on your goals and exactly what you want. It helps you with focus and clarity. Glenn is a very generous guy who has nothing to prove – he's secure within himself. He said to me that based on year-by-year achievements, we're in the same place in business development – except that he is ten years ahead. I enjoy our friendship and the fact that we can talk over a glass of wine and diagnose and improve each others' businesses.

It's a really exciting thing – like a factory for ideas, a two-way flow. It's great to be able to do that. The strategies he teaches on the advanced part of his course were the ones that were most effective for me. With his support, I quadrupled the size of my business in four years and have trebled it in the last three years. One of the greatest drivers of that success has been to fully take on board everything that Glenn teaches.

So that's my advice to someone who is considering working with him as a mentor: spend as much time as you can with him and do everything that he says. This may well mean moving out of your comfort zone, and so you may notice resistance in yourself, but get over it and just move forward. Glenn's a formidable character and even with the experience I had, I was a little scared of where that would take me. He asks you to have a vision for your future, and as well as excitement, that can bring up fear.

Another thing that Glenn and I definitely have in common is a love of personal development. Glenn actively promotes a reading list of personal development books, which is something that resonates with me. Something very interesting which emerged as we became friends is that we both experienced times as young children where we felt a sense of fragility.

I knew when I was quite small that my mother was under stress because she didn't have enough money. I remember how that was, and my wish to help her and change everything, but not being able to because I was only a child. To this day, I still send my mother money so that she doesn't have to worry.

I remember very clearly the sense that money is like oxygen: you don't need to go around collecting it when you have enough – but if you lack it, it's as though you are suffocating. Glenn's experience is different but has an interesting similarity. He has asthma as a child and experienced a real struggle with that. He knows the feeling of fighting for one breath at a time, and how it teaches you the value of life.

The spiritual side of life is important to me. Neale Donald Walsch wrote a *book called Conversations with God that changed the way I experienced life forever. I've also been influenced by Eckhart Tolle's The Power of Now and by Robert Kiyosaki's Rich Dad Poor Dad. That was what helped clarify in my mind that it was okay for me to be entrepreneurial – that this was something natural to me and that I could use the qualities I had in a positive way. My dad was in the TV repairing business in the 70s and by the time I was 16, I was driving one of the nicest cars in school because I had a portfolio of rental TVs as well as a trading business in repairing TVs. Rich Dad Poor Dad helped me to recognise myself, and be okay with who I am.*

I would cite Glenn as right up there with those writers as one of those major influences of my life. He's so strong on personal development that in his brain he carries the themes and ideas of many of these books and integrates them into his life and work. He's able to summon up the right thing at the right time. I had a very unusual experience with him once: I ended up being part of a taped consultation with him, and when it was played back to me I was able to hear myself blustering and being held back by my fear. I didn't recognise that person on the recording as really being me – perhaps I didn't want to. But I resolved from that moment on to just to be a lot clearer in my mind, and a lot more present in acting on Glenn's strategies.

The reality for me is I would have made it anyway. I'm the type of person that I will climb the mountain regardless. But Glenn's made the journey more enjoyable and more fun... and he's certainly made it quicker.

Says Glenn:

Ian has gone from £10,000 a month when he first joined me to £40,000 a month profit which will soon be increasing to £50,000 a month.

Jason Rounce

Before I met Glenn, I was working in property in the most practical way possible – I was a builder! I did an apprenticeship as a brick layer then worked my way up from there, and I'd worked on a few development projects. It was satisfying work and I'd been doing it for 30 years. But I'd never managed a project independently, and I was definitely feeling ready to go on to greater things.

I've always had a belief in my ability to create something special. I was quite driven, and I wanted to do the best possible job. When I was building, I paid a lot of attention to details and finishes. I realised that my approach and my experience would stand me in good stead. But I also realised that I had to add knowledge: I had to learn how to find deals, identify suitable properties and manage the finances.

I met Glenn in September 2014. It was a very painful and difficult time in my life, because in March I had lost my wife to breast cancer. My son was doing his GCSEs and my daughter was in her first year at university, living away from home after recently losing her mother. So I was trying to be strong for both my children. But it was very hard because I'd also lost my rock, the woman I always used to turn to when I was stressed or having problems or had had a bad day at work. To be really honest, it was frightening to be without her love and support.

I truly think that was one of the things that inspired me to go on Glenn's course. I had a very strong sense that I must move forward now. I'd been on his email list for about 5 years after I heard him speak in Norwich, and from time to time I'd see the emails pop up, but I'd never taken any action. Then, when I lost my wife, I put a house that we'd owned together on the market, and as a result I had a lump sum of £110,000. I didn't want it to go to waste – and I knew my wife wouldn't have wanted that either. And if you just start spending money – buy a car, buy a holiday, buy a new kitchen… suddenly, it can be gone.

So I decided the money was going to go into property. My first idea was to buy a few little terraced houses, do them up and rent them out. I went to an auction and I bought one. Then I thought I'd buy a few more… but before I did, it was time to go on Glenn's course. And what I learned there really changed things for me.

The course was mind blowing. It really, really was. The first day was all about setting your goals and why you were on the course. The big question Glenn asks is… what is your why? What's your inspiration for being on the course, and what you want to achieve? People gave different answers – I'm doing it for my children's future, they said, or because I haven't got a pension, or because I don't like my job.

But my 'why?' was different. Mine was because I was frightened. I was on my own, having to look after my children, and I didn't have anyone to fall back. I knew that they needed me more than ever and I had to be there for them. So I wanted to be in charge of how I spent my time, not be tied to working on someone else's schedule. If my children needed me, I wanted to be available.

The second day of the course was about finding the right deals. It covered building up relationships with professionals – estate agents, surveyors, architects – and knowing how to speak in the language of those professions so that you can get business done. The third day was all about deal structuring, putting different types of deals together. This was the real Eureka moment for me. It was as if Glenn had switched a light on. I'd done lots of work for people with big property portfolios and I'd never understood how they financed what they were doing. I felt as though I was soaking up knowledge like a sponge.

Glenn calls the fourth day 'head mash day'. That's because he throws so many different strategies at you, and teaches you a lot about body language and how important it is for communication. He shared the story of his own background and how he became successful in business – how he built up his video business then lost everything, and then bounced back.

I could really relate to that, because in 2000 I had a limited company in a holiday camp go into liquidation, owing me £180,000. So I had to declare myself personally bankrupt, but I bounced back from that too. I could totally understand where Glenn was coming from. It's all about your mindset – not about what happens to you, but about how you respond. Glenn's also very good at reading what's going on in a situation, and knowing when you need to do something creative to grab someone's attention. I just thought – wow, I can see how this guy's been so successful.

I joined the Mentorship and Mastermind Programme. Quite a few of us from the course did. And yet a year and half later, there were only about 3 people from our course still there. I remember finding it strange that people who had been so enthusiastic at the time hadn't followed through. But it's one thing to gain knowledge and another thing to put that knowledge into action. Not everyone is prepared to take action. Glenn's a man of action. He knows a lot about theory and strategy, but in the end, success is about what you do.

For me, Glenn's mentorship has provided the support structure I needed to be able to take that action. It's like a bit of a safety net – there's advice and help for you when you need it. And of course, Glenn is a role model. I have a lot of admiration for him. When someone who has done it himself is telling you that you can do it too – you believe that you can.

Now back to that first little terraced house I'd bought. Glenn said to me – you've got to sell it. And I thought, I don't want to sell it – I only just bought it! But he explained about deal financing and how important it was to plan ahead and build up a cash fund to to pay deposits to build up my portfolio. This kind of strategic thinking really made sense to me and changed the way I approached things. Thanks to him, I became far more professional.

The other thing about the 4-day course that really impressed me was that Glenn tries to give everyone at least 10 minutes of his time, one-to-one. When we spoke, he wanted to find out what situation I was in life, what financial place I was in, so that he could give me the specific help and advice I needed. There are people on the course at many different stages of their journey in property, and I liked that attention to individuals who might have very different needs.

The master mind programme involves a monthly meeting. It gives you access to Glenn and the other people in his power networking team and that's been inspirational. The practical help and advice is absolutely worth its weight in gold. You set yourself goals to achieve each month. You hear about what other people are doing and learn by that. And you also see them taking action, so it gives you a benchmark for your progress and encourages you to keep moving forward.

I've been inspired by Glenn to make a difference to my life and my family's life. Every penny I spent on the programme has been well spent. It's been a game-changer. I remember Glenn talking about musicians. The ones that practice 3 or 4 hours a day are okay. The ones that practice 8 hours a day are good, but they're middle-of-the-road. It's the ones that practice 12 hours a day who are really at the top of their game. So if I'm going to do this and make a success of it, I've got to seriously commit my time to it.

If you're serious about a career in property too – go on the course, learn from Glenn and take in everything you possibly can. Definitely join the mentorship programme... and make Glenn's life a misery. Phone him up, text him, ask him questions, make that investment work for you. Because – it will do. He's there to help, he wants to help you and he's got such a lot of knowledge.

I'm in a fantastic place at the moment. I love getting up in the mornings now. I look forward to what the day brings and to building what I've started to create into something bigger and better.

I have a new partner too – Angie. I've found happiness in my life again, which is a wonderful thing. I'm truly grateful to the people who've helped me move forward, and most of all to Glenn.

Says Glenn

"Jason is one of my most successful students. When he started with me I asked him to sell his one buy-to-let property, which he did to raise £80,000. He followed my advice and is currently on target to turn that into £1.1m within three years of being on the course."

Lynne Moran

I'd been working in property for some time in Scotland, and had gained quite a lot of experience in management and refurbishment. Then, in 2008, my husband and I moved south – to Buckinghamshire. The property world there was very different, with much higher prices, so the model of business I had worked in before was problematic.

I found a job in property that I enjoyed, but I missed my independence as a businesswoman. I realised that to work for myself in the future, I needed to grow my skills and knowledge and adapt to a new environment.

I went to a meeting held in Maidenhead where Glenn was giving a talk. away I was impressed – but I'm naturally cautious and wanted to find out more. We spoke afterwards and he didn't push anything onto me – in fact he was very laid-back. He suggested that I should gather more information. I really liked that approach – it made me feel confident right from the start.

A few days later I received an email with details about his four day course. I weighed it up carefully and my husband and I both decided to attend.

The course was held in central London and it turned out to be quite an eye-opener. Something that Glenn said when we first met had really resonated with me: "you don't know what you don't know". Of course I was aware of gaps in my knowledge, but at the same time, the course gave me confidence that I could learn.

What I hadn't been involved in before was creative property development – my clients had always been the ones who were doing the purchasing. Now I discovered the real skills and strategies needed for putting together a deal. That's what you need these days if you're going to make a success of a property career.

On day two – halfway through the programme – I had made my decision that this was for me. My husband felt the same and we joined Glenn's partnership programme together. I threw myself right in straightaway and began to attend the regular meetings. There are two levels for people starting out – one is for total beginners who are learning the business from scratch, but Glenn recommended that I start at the higher level because of the previous experience I had.

From the very beginning, my decision felt right for three reasons: the first was the content of the programme I was on. It was very hands-on – totally grounded in the real world and actual business experience. The education got started right away, and all the time you are working with and learning from people – Glenn himself of course most of all – who have been there and done it. You're with like-minded investors, discussing their real-life situations with Glenn's creative input. He listens very carefully then helps people find a solution to whatever the issue might be. It's a powerful way to gain understanding.

The second reason was Glenn himself – he's a very funny person and that was important to me. We had quite a few giggles and I liked his whole persona. I'd realised that I needed a mentor - someone I respected and could enjoy working with and learning from. So I wanted one who matched my personality. If you're going to dedicate your time to a project, it helps a lot to be around people who are on the same wavelength.

The third thing was really important to me – the flexibility the programme can offer. If you're a natural risk-taker (and I know that some *people are) you can give up the day job and just throw yourself in and build a new property career. I'm not the sort of person who takes huge chances, so right now I still have a full-time job and I've begun to grow my property portfolio around that.*

For me it has been stepping stones and that is what has suited me best. There's no one right way to do it, and you'll never be pressured to take any step you're not fully prepared for.

Working full-time alongside the programme means I have made the decision to set aside some time, at evenings and weekends, to do the necessary work. It's important to be disciplined about this – I'm very busy, but it's something I prioritise. I also enjoy it very much and I of course, I've gained so much from doing it.

On Glenn's programme, finding suitable properties is up to you. You need to get out there and apply what you've learned. I was successful quite quickly – four weeks after starting, I found a property I thought would really work. Next I took my idea along to a meeting, where everyone proposes their plans for other members to see and learn from.

Glenn listens while you set out what you are intending to do, and makes suggestions. He's always positive in his approach, but straightforward: if he sees a problem he will say so. His insights and experience are so valuable and constructive. In my case, he gave the thumbs-up, so I went ahead and made the deal.

I like everyone involved in the partnership programme – I can honestly say that I feel I have inherited a whole family. We have a lot of fun, but we're learning all the time. There's a lot of respect for one another – no-one would do anything surreptitious and the whole thing is highly professional. That's reflected in the fact that programme members will often do business together, forming joint ventures so that we can draw on each others' expertise.

I have made new friends, and my property career is developing well. I am now in the process of making two land deals. I'm very excited about what the future holds in store. Glenn's programme offers amazing opportunities to people that are passionate.

My advice to others would be to make sure this is really what you want to do– just throw yourself in. That was the point I reached on day two of Glenn's course. It felt right, it made sense – so take action.

I've gained so much that I've offered my time to speak at some of Glenn's courses. I can advise other people in exactly the position I was in myself: I know what it's like to be sitting there, and just what they are thinking and how they are feeling. It's great to be speaking to them about my journey and the support I've had.

If someone had said to me back then that I'd be up there, doing this myself and giving my own presentation – I would have been astonished. But I think that I can be a good role model to others, and I'm delighted that my input has been very well received.

What makes Glenn different is the lack of hard sell – which I think is really based on quiet confidence. I do receive emails from other investors in the UK who offer training, and his in-depth knowledge, and of course his experience, really make him really stand out. When you present Glenn with a problem, you see the cogs ticking over, but I've never seen him stumped. He always makes a great suggestions, and that's very reassuring. Glenn has a solution, whatever the problem might be. He inspired me, and I can honestly say from the moment that I started working with him, I have never looked back.

Says Glenn:

"Lynn is on target to make £420,000 profit from her first two deals. Both of them are delayed completions on plots where we first obtain planning consent and then build the property. The land is paid for after the property is built. Here total outlay is just over £20,000 as 100% development finance is being used."

*"Read, every day, something
no one else is reading.
Think, every day, something
no one else is thinking.
Do, every day, something
no one else would be
silly enough to do.
It is bad for the mind to
continually be part of unanimity."*

Christopher Morley

Chapter Fifteen

Glenn's recommended reading list

If you want to become a millionaire, you will need to think like a millionaire. This means feeding your mind with the sort of information you will need to develop your success mindset. Your previous mindset has got you this far, but if you want to go further, you need to be reprogrammed.

They say that if you want to know what lies ahead on the road, ask someone coming towards you. I have always been a reader and hungry to learn. I realise that there is not enough time to make all the mistakes myself, but if I can learn from the mistakes and the insights of others, it is going to save me a lot of time.

But before sharing my list with you, do remember that reading these books is something you do after you have taken the necessary actions you need to do for your business. Do not use them as an excuse for putting things off.

I have noticed that, with some of my mentees, they have got 'caught in the headlights' with information overload and have not acted as a result. If you feel this way, then we need to talk. That is what a mentor is for.

The more you act, the more confidence you will get and the easier things will be. I am always here to make sure that you don't make any foolish mistakes.

Think and Grow Rich

Probably the most important book that I read early on was Napoleon Hill's classic *Think and Grow Rich*. You need to read it! Interestingly, although the book dates back to 1937, the fundamental 'laws' and philosophies he writes about have never been bettered, and indeed, many later writers and motivational speakers have reworked them and made good careers out of training them.

Hill laid the foundations of his book in his first work *The Law of Success in Sixteen Lessons* which he was commissioned to write by Dale Carnegie.

The book was based on a series of interviews of over 100 American millionaires across nearly 20 years, including such self-made industrial giants as Henry Ford, J. P. Morgan, John D. Rockefeller, Alexander Graham Bell, and Thomas Edison.

To tap into the thinking of these great minds is invaluable and well worth the effort of getting yourself a copy.

The book starts with a great principle – learn from a mastermind and a mentor. Work with someone who has done it first. Next, 'Know very clearly where you want to go,' your personal vision and goals are key. There are 13 steps in the book and all of them solid gold.

Think and Grow Rich followed and was published in the middle of America's Great Depression and gave hope and inspiration to countless thousand of people. It has gone on to sell over 100 million copies. Make it 100 million and one! The same advice applies to Dale Carnegie's book *How to Win Friends and Influence People*, first published in 1936. The principles it contains formed the basis of a personal development course which went worldwide and is still being delivered today

Twelve Things This Book Will Do For You
(An extract from *How to Win Friends and Influence People* by Dale Carnegie)

- Get you out of a mental rut, give you new thoughts, new visions, new ambitions.
- Enable you to make friends quickly and easily.
- Increase your popularity.
- Help you to win people to your way of thinking.
- Increase your influence, your prestige, your ability to get things done.
- Enable you to win new clients, new customers.
- Increase your earning power.
- Make you a better salesman, a better executive.
- Help you to handle complaints, avoid arguments, keep your human contacts smooth and pleasant.
- Make you a better speaker, a more entertaining conversationalist.
- Make the principles of psychology easy for you to apply in your daily contacts.
- Help you to arouse enthusiasm among your associates.

If that doesn't persuade you to buy it, I don't know what will. If not, it is available as a free download! What's keeping you?

"First comes thought;
then organization of that thought,
into ideas and plans;
then transformation of
those plans into reality.
The beginning,
as you will observe,
is in your imagination."

Napoleon Hill

Rich Dad, Poor Dad - financial literacy

A lot of what I was taught at school has never been of great value in my life. Nobody has ever asked me to recite the 17 times table. The only thing I remember from geography is the difference between stalagmites and stalactites – tights come down.

What they never taught us was the most important skill of financial literacy. As a result, whole generations grow up struggling with credit card debt and the challenge of too much month at the end of the money. A little knowledge goes a long way.

That is why I was so impressed with Robert Kiyosaki and his book *Rich Dad, Poor Dad*. Robert is passionate about helping people get to grip with the world of money, something you will need to be very good at!

Kiyosaki is known for simplifying complex concepts and ideas related to business, investing, finance and economics. He has grown an international reputation for his straight talking, irreverence, courage, and views on money and investing that often contradicts conventional financial advice.

No matter how good you think you are with money, this book is well worth reading and is full of golden nuggets.

The book was originally self-published in 1997 before being picked up commercially to become a New York Times bestseller. It has since sold 26 million copies and become a household name. In his audiobook, *Choose to be rich*, Kiyosaki said that every publisher turned him down, and Barnes & Noble refused to stock the book initially. He placed his focus on talk shows and radio show appearances, of which *The Oprah Winfrey Show* had the biggest influence on book sales. Many of my mentees talk about how powerful this book was for them.

"Real estate investing,
even on a very small scale,
remains a tried and true
means of building
an individual's
cash flow
and wealth."

Robert Kiyosaki

The 7 Habits of Highly Effective People

Stephen R. Covey's bestselling book is also on my essential reading list. *The 7 Habits of Highly Effective People*, first published in 1989, is a business and self-help book in which he presents an approach to being effective in attaining goals by aligning oneself to what he calls 'true north' principles of a character ethic that he presents as universal and timeless.

Covey's book has sold more than 25 million copies worldwide since its publication in 1989. The audio version became the first non-fiction audio book in the USA publishing history to sell more than one million copies. Covey argues against what he calls 'The Personality Ethic', something he sees as prevalent in many modern self-help books. He promotes what he labels 'The Character Ethic': aligning one's values with so-called 'universal and timeless' principles.

Covey adamantly refuses to conflate principles and values; he sees principles as external natural laws, while values remain internal and subjective. Covey proclaims that values govern people's behaviour, but principles ultimately determine the consequences. Covey presents his teachings in a series of habits, manifesting as a progression from dependence via independence to interdependence.

*"When you show deep
empathy toward others,
their defensive energy goes down,
and positive energy replaces it.
That's when you can get
more creative in solving problems."*

Stephen R. Covey

The Richest Man in Babylon

I believe that the most important life lesson is contained in this book. It is an absolute classic! Written by George Samuel Clason, the book dispenses financial advice through a collection of parables set in ancient Babylon.

Through their experiences in business and managing household finance, the characters in the parables learn simple lessons in financial wisdom. Originally a series of separate informational pamphlets distributed by banks and insurance companies, the pamphlets were bound together and published in book form in 1926. I believe that it is still as valuable today as it was when it was first published. For example:

The Five Laws of Gold

Kalabab relates the story of a man named Nomasir (The son of Arkad, The Richest Man in Babylon), who went out to make his way in the world. He foolishly lost the money that his father had given to him, but remembered the five laws of gold that his father had related to him.

- Gold cometh gladly and in increasing quantity to any man who will put by not less than one-tenth of his earnings to create an estate for his future and that of his family. (Save 10% of your gross earnings.)

- Gold laboreth diligently and contentedly for the wise owner who finds for it profitable employment, multiplying even as the flocks of the field.

- Gold clingeth to the protection of the cautious owner who invests it under the advice of men wise in its handling.

- Gold slippeth away from the man who invests it in businesses or purposes with which he is not familiar or which are not approved by those skilled in its keep. (Educate yourself or rely on those who are educated in the investment you're interested in.)

- Gold flees the man who would force it to impossible earnings or who followeth the alluring advice of tricksters and schemers or who trusts it to his own inexperience and romantic desires in investment.

Kalabab then relates that, using these laws of gold, Nomasir became rich. "Yet, who can measure in bags of gold, the value of wisdom? Without wisdom, gold is quickly lost by those who have it, but with wisdom, gold can be secured by those who have it not, as these three bags of gold do prove."

The Art of the Deal

For all the publicity that he is currently getting, it is easy to forget that Donald Trump has enjoyed amazing success in business. His 1987 book *Trump: The Art of the Deal* is part-memoir and part-business advice book. It reached number one on the New York Times bestseller list and held a position on the list for 51 weeks. It was the first book published by Trump and helped to make him a "household name".

The book received additional attention during Trump's 2016 campaign for the presidency of the United States. He cited it as one of his proudest accomplishments, and his second favourite book (after the Bible).

The book tells about Trump's childhood, his work in Brooklyn prior to moving to Manhattan and building The Trump Organization out of his studio apartment, developing the Hyatt Hotels and Trump Tower, renovating Wollman Rink, and other projects.

The book also contains an 11-step formula for business success inspired by Norman Vincent Peale's *The Power of Positive Thinking*. The steps include No. 11 "Think Big", No. 7 "Get the Word Out", and No. 10 "Contain the Costs".

*"I like thinking big.
If you're going to
be thinking anything,
you might as well
think big."*

Donald Trump

Feel the fear and do it anyway

No personal development library would be complete without *Feel the Fear and Do It Anyway*. Internationally renowned author Susan Jeffers has helped millions of people around the globe to overcome their fears and heal the pain in their lives.

Susan Jeffers was born Susan Gildenberg at Hazleton, Pennsylvania on March 3, 1938. She started her academic education at Penn State University, but abandoned her studies when she married her first husband. In the years following 1960, the family moved to Manhattan, where Jeffers took degrees, followed by a doctorate in psychology, at Hunter College and at Columbia University.

In 1971, Susan Jeffers became executive director of the Floating Hospital in New York. She then taught a course about fear at the New School for Social Research.

She published her first and presumably most well-known self-help book *Feel the Fear and Do It Anyway* in 1987. It was sold in millions of copies and translated into more than 35 languages. In addition to her work as an author, Jeffers also held workshops and seminars.

In her book and seminars, she addressed such fears may include: public speaking; asserting yourself; making decisions; intimacy; changing jobs; being alone; ageing; driving; losing a loved one; and ending a relationship.

But whatever your anxieties, *Feel the Fear and Do It Anyway* will give you the insight and tools to vastly improve your ability to handle any given situation. You will learn to live your life the way you want, so you can move from a place of pain, paralysis and depression to one of power, energy and enthusiasm.

This inspiring modern classic has helped thousands turn their anger into love – and their indecision into action – with Susan Jeffers' simple but profound advice to 'feel the fear and do it anyway'.

"Fear stifles our thinking and actions.
It creates indecisiveness
that results in stagnation.
I have known talented people who
procrastinate indefinitely
rather than risk failure.
Lost opportunities cause
erosion of confidence,
and the downward spiral begins."

Charles Stanley

The Naked Ape: A Zoologist's Study of the Human Animal

You may be surprised at my choice of this book, but it is very insightful. With your property business, you will be dealing with all sorts of people. Understanding what makes them tick and being able to read they way they are feeling by understanding their body language is essential.

In this book, you will meet the Naked Ape at his most primal – in love, at work, at war. Meet man as he really is: relative to the apes, stripped of his veneer as we see him courting, making love, sleeping, socialising, grooming and playing.

Zoologist Desmond Morris' classic takes its place alongside Darwin's *The Origin of the Species*, presenting man not as a fallen angel, but as a risen ape, remarkable in his resilience, energy and imagination, yet an animal nonetheless, in danger of forgetting his origins. With its penetrating insights on man's beginnings, sex life, habits and our astonishing bonds to the animal kingdom, *The Naked Ape* is a landmark, at once provocative, compelling and timeless.

*"Body language is
a very powerful tool.
We had body language
before we had speech,
and apparently, 80%
of what you understand
in a conversation is
read through the body,
not the words."*

Deborah Bull

Influence: The Psychology of Persuasion

This is my last book recommendation to help you to improve your ability to negotiate.

Influence, the classic book on persuasion, explains the psychology of why people say "yes" – and how to apply these understandings.

Dr. Robert Cialdini is the seminal expert in the rapidly expanding field of influence and persuasion. His 35 years of rigorous, evidence-based research along with a three-year programme of study on what moves people to change behaviour, has resulted in this highly acclaimed book.

Dr. Cialdini received his Bachelor of Science degree from the University of Wisconsin in June 1967. He then went on to graduate studies in Social Psychology at the University of North Carolina and earned his Ph.D. in June 1970 and received Postgraduate training in Social Psychology at Columbia University. He has held Visiting Scholar Appointments at Ohio State University, the University of California, the Annenberg School of Communications, and the Graduate School of Business of Stanford University. Currently, Dr. Cialdini is Regents' Professor Emeritus of Psychology and Marketing at Arizona State University

In this book, you'll learn the six universal principles, how to use them to become a skilled persuader – and how to defend yourself against them. Perfect for people in all walks of life, the principles of *Influence* will move you towards profound personal change and act as a driving force for your success. You will learn a lot from this one!

The book has sold over three million copies and has been translated into 30 languages. It has been listed on the New York Times Business Bestseller List. Fortune Magazine lists the book in their "75 Smartest Business Books".

His two other books, *Yes! 50 Scientifically Proven Ways to Be Persuasive* and *The Small BIG: Small changes that spark a big influence* were a New York Times Bestseller and The Times Book of the Year respectively.

"Rhetoric may be defined as the faculty of observing in any given case the available means of persuasion. This is not a function of any other art."

Aristotle

Chapter Sixteen
Conclusion

In this book, I have shared my story, the things I have learned on my journey, and the main strategies that I have used to build my £45 million (and growing) property portfolio. You have all the knowledge you need to become a property millionaire yourself. What happens next is up to you. If knowledge was all it takes to become rich, Oxford dons would be driving Ferraris, not bicycles! It is not about know, but about action. It is the action you take next that will be what counts.

How is it that I can stand at the front of the room and talk to a group of people, but only a small handful use the information I have shared with them to take the first steps to build their property portfolio?

These days, with little or no return from putting savings in the bank, more and more people are discovering that, despite all the ups and downs of the marketplace, property is still the most predictable way of getting a regular return.

There is a world of opportunity out there. There are properties waiting for you. There's an increasing number every day of people looking for somewhere to live. If you don't put your knowledge into action, then you can be certain that someone else will.

But a word of caution. One thing I have noticed is that each one of the 69 people that I have mentored to become equity millionaires has done it slightly differently. This is not 'one size fits all'.

When I mentor people, it is with the intention of helping them to develop a strategy that is tailored to their personality, skills and individual requirements, rather than moulding them into one way of working.

My advice to you is to come to one of my one-day taster events and find out for yourself. Come and talk to others who have been on my programmes and find out their experiences. I look forward to meeting you and opening the door to the most rewarding new career you could ever hope to find.

If we work together, I can show you how to go from zero to £100,000 in 12 to 18 months. Building on that, I can then show you how to go from £100,000 to £1 million in three to five years. I have done this countless times, as you will see from the testimonials at the back of this book. If you have got what it takes, are prepared to listen and to take actions, there is absolutely no reason why you could enjoy that same success yourself.

Glenn

www.glennarmstrong.com

Private Clients

I take on a limited number of private clients, working with only four at any one time. This gives me the opportunity of providing more personal attention and access to my diary. This is what one of my private clients has said:

"I feel compelled to write this testimonial for Glenn Armstrong and his mentoring programme. I first went on a one-day, £500 training course with Glenn around five years ago. Since then, I have been absolutely amazed at the number of transactions that I have been able to complete as a consequence of the knowledge and skills that I gleaned from that day. I estimate it to have resulted in above £200,000 in profit!

"At the end of last year, I reviewed my portfolio and progress towards my goals and realised that I wanted to be progressing towards them much faster than I currently was. I am a full-time investor with a portfolio of over 40 properties, but I have a huge desire to house the homeless and having set up a franchise to do just that, I was frustrated at the rate of growth of this project and the low numbers of disadvantaged people we were housing each night.

"So I again turned to Glenn. I attended his four-day course in London (a little sceptically, if I'm honest, as I'd expected it to be around £2,000 but it was only £400!). The value from this four days is absolutely

huge, tens of thousands of pounds without a doubt (I've done two transactions in the month since as a direct result of my learning from those four days). I also decided to join Glenn's mentorship programme and if I'm honest this has, and I can see will continue to, transform my business. I have just finished a three-day trip with Glenn around the south of England visiting some current transactions of his. I don't think it's an exaggeration to say that from every hour I spent listening, watching and being mentored by Glenn, I learned something new.

"'Little' things, like how:

- *I can save £18,000 off my annual refurbishment bills by investing one hour of my time once;*
- *I can pay myself £30,000 extra tax-free each year than I currently am;*
- *to negotiate a purchase and build a deal using none of my own money that makes £1m profit;*
- *to improve the quality and number of my power team around me (solicitors, valuers, insurance brokers, builders, architects, mortgage brokers etc.); and,*
- *to completely legally avoid section 106 and CIS payments when developing large numbers of units.*

"To be honest, I have tens of pages of pure gold learnings like these above that I am so grateful to have been shown and taught since returning to Glenn's education programme.

"There is no one that I'm aware of who knows their stuff better in the UK.

"No one who teaches others, but predominantly makes their money from DOING what they teach in property (this is very rare, in my experience).

"And no one (who I know, at least) in this industry who genuinely wants to take your money and deliver ten times the value you're expecting.

"This has certainly been my experience with Glenn and the reason that I can wholeheartedly recommend him. A massive thank you to Glenn and the Glenn Armstrong team."

Frank Flegg
Co-founder of Stepping Stones, the not-for-profit project that is ending homelessness globally.

"We found it fantastic! We came here to learn more strategies and definitely did! It was an eye-opener because it made us look at our recent deals we have done, and we could have made more money on them if we knew of the knowledge we learned this weekend. Thank you very much, Glenn and the team. Outstanding!"

Nick and Paul Curley

"I'm a partner in a very low energy building and property development company in south-east London. We specialise in transforming run-down properties into funky, stylish homes by adding value through, extensions re: configuration and new builds in gardens. Love this kind of strategy and will combine with lease options, delayed completions and assignable contracts."

Claire Hunte

"I'm newish to property; parents are investors and I have been shadowing my dad the last few months. I came here for the education to help be a more effective part of the collective business as a family, but also to launch myself forward in my own right moving at a faster pace than I am investing with my parents.

"I enjoyed learning all the strategies and having my mind opened to what is possible and what I can achieve.

"Prior to attending, I had renovated a house and sold it on and thought I'd continue in the same way, but although I may still do this, my mind has expanded to new ideas. For that, I am grateful. Thank you. Much needed inspiration."

David Mobbs

"My experience in property is limited, very much a starter. The course has given me the potential to use many different methods to help me achieve my goal of £10,000 per month in three years. Glenn clearly has huge experience and an excellent problem-solving brain. I look forward to this mentorship programme and working with Glenn and making me, Glenn and future partners lots of money! And having fun."

Tim Edwards

"I have learnt more than I ever imagined I would. I have done a few property training courses in the past and thought I knew enough to build a successful property portfolio, and cash flow enough money to be financially free. Now that I have been educated by Glenn, I now realise I was lacking the correct information to achieve significant success. I would recommend this course to anyone who is serious about property."

Patricia Minnell

"I am a small investor with a portfolio of 13 units. I've been investing for 20 years but need to get up to the next level as the traditional way of investing has bogged me down."

Dee Bell

"I've been site construction manager on large one-off developments with values of £3 million plus. I've been surrounded by developers 24/7 for two years. I have learned more in four days and have seen how much my employers have been leaving on the table. I love how personal the whole team are and actually can't believe how quick the whole course went. It has given me and the whole class an awesome experience."

Frank McNicholl

"I enjoyed the four-day property intensive, very informative. I work full-time (four days on, four days off) so have a lot of time to invest. I have a property that is let out. I am very much interesting in flipping and rent to rent."

Ken Sokhal

"My goal is to turn £100,000 into £1 million within three to five years, and by putting into place everything I have learned on the course and with Glenn's help, I now believe that goal is achievable.

"The course and Glenn teaches so much more than any other course I have been on and I would highly recommend it to anyone looking to be successful in property."

Jemma Edwards

"As a person who has worked in the property industry for seven years, I was surprised by how much new information I was provided by the course. Not only was it informative, but very enjoyable and Glenn was an entertaining person to learn from. I would have no concerns in recommending others to have his courses and I will certainly be back for further education."

Matthew Ballard

"I am a novice investor. I just bought my first property in March. I first saw Glenn when he was speaking at the Berkshire Property Meet. I knew there and then that he was the right mentor for me.

"I came on the four-day property course and he blew my mind with his crazy but very legal property strategies that I'd never ever heard of before. I can't wait for my mentorship programme over the next 18 months. I'm going to be one of his first 100 property millionaires."

Oleesha Minnell

"I am a lettings agent/deal sourcer, now doing rent to rent. I give this course a high rating. Very informative, everything broken down very clearly."

Jade Valentine

"I'm 17 but have been around property all my life. Glenn is a genius at finding money in a potential deal with strategies that are so simple, yet you wouldn't think of."

Caleb Lacey

"Huge advantage, strategies, networking contacts. Great four-day event. Thank you."

Safdar R Khan

"I am an interior designer with a background in psychology. I came on this course to better understand the financial side of property and what is possible. My mind has definitely been blown. Even with property developer parents, I didn't realise how many different strategies there are. Glenn has intensive knowledge of the latest and most creative ways of doings. I really enjoyed broadening my understanding of the business and learning a variety of techniques and strategies."

Victoria Mobbs

"Very good four days of training. I learned some new ways of doing things and made some great contacts. Really worth the money and time."

Mark Climments

"WOW! Brain very full. Want and need more info. I can't wait to start the mentorship programme, partnership programme and also to do a day on the rent-to-rent programme. I am planning to find out what I can do next, which will help me get to the next level. Thank you very much and I look forward to working with you."

Sean Reuben

"Well, what can we say other than 'bloody marvellous'. You really don't know what you don't know until you attend the four-day course with Glenn. We run a construction company; Adi has 25 years of experience in the building trade and I have a background in H&S and now run a network marketing company. The knowledge we have gained today is priceless and I am confident it will accelerate our success to levels we may have only previously dreamt of. Big thanks to Glenn and the team."

Chrissy & Adi Wright

"I'm a property investor with three houses and 14 rentals. I have a lettings agency and estate agency. These four-days have been brilliant. Glenn has focused my brain, given me strategies to make more money and made me realise the business I am in. Thank you! See you soon."

Andy Geldar

Space for notes and questions

Space for notes and questions

Space for notes and questions